The
PURSUIT OF YOUR EXCELLENCE

Napoleon Hill (1883–1970), best known for his global bestseller *Think and Grow Rich*, was a self-help author and businessman whose work has influenced millions across the world, from Norman Vincent Peale to Donald Trump. Born poor, Hill lived a colourful life, pursuing several different business ventures and professions. He also met and advised many famous people, such as US President Woodrow Wilson. Hill eventually found widespread success as a motivational author, writing several books on how to achieve success and practically creating the self-help genre.

The
PURSUIT OF YOUR EXCELLENCE

How to Build a ***Successful*** *and* ***Fulfilling Life***

NAPOLEON HILL

RUPA

Published by
Rupa Publications India Pvt. Ltd 2024
7/16, Ansari Road, Daryaganj
New Delhi 110002

Sales centres:
Bengaluru Chennai
Hyderabad Jaipur Kathmandu
Kolkata Mumbai Prayagraj

Edition copyright © Rupa Publications India Pvt. Ltd 2024

All rights reserved.
No part of this publication may be reproduced, transmitted,
or stored in a retrieval system, in any form or by any means, electronic,
mechanical, photocopying, recording or otherwise, without the prior
permission of the publisher.

P-ISBN: 978-93-5702-705-2
E-ISBN: 978-93-5702-851-6

First impression 2024

10 9 8 7 6 5 4 3 2 1

Printed in India

This book is sold subject to the condition that it shall not, by way of
trade or otherwise, be lent, resold, hired out, or otherwise circulated,
without the publisher's prior consent, in any form of binding or
cover other than that in which it is published.

CONTENTS

1. The Twelve Riches of Life — 7
2. The Master Mind Group—a Power Beyond Science — 17
3. Initiative and Leadership — 33
4. Accurate Thought — 39
5. Tolerance — 52
6. Habit of Doing More than Paid For — 72
7. Maintain Sound Health — 88
8. Learn from Adversity and Defeat — 102
9. Wisdom Robs Death of Its Sting — 112
10. The Sixth Sense — 116
11. It Is Upto You to Live the Life the Creator Gave You — 129

1

THE TWELVE RICHES OF LIFE

The greatest of all riches is…

1. A POSITIVE MENTAL ATTITUDE

All riches, of whatsoever nature, begin as a state of mind; and let us remember that a state of mind is the one and only thing over which any person has complete, unchallenged right of control.

It is highly significant that the Creator provided man with control over nothing except the power to shape his own thoughts and the privilege of fitting them to any pattern of his choice.

Mental attitude is important because it converts the brain into the equivalent of an electro-magnet which attracts the counterpart of one's dominating thoughts, aims and purposes. It also attracts the counterpart of one's fears, worries and doubts.

A positive mental attitude is the starting point of all riches, whether they be riches of a material nature or intangible riches.

It attracts the riches of true friendship.

And the riches one finds in the hope of future achievement.

It provides the riches one may find in Nature's handiwork, as it exists in the moonlit nights, in the stars that float out there in the heavens, in the beautiful landscapes and in distant horizons.

And the riches to be found in the labor of one's choice, where expression may be given to the highest plane of man's soul.

And the riches of harmony in home relationships, where all members of the family work together in a spirit of friendly cooperation.

And the riches of sound physical health, which is the treasure of those who have learned to balance work with play, worship with love, and who have learned the wisdom of eating to live rather than of living to eat.

And the riches of freedom from fear.

And the riches of enthusiasm, both active and passive.

And the riches of song and laughter, both of which indicate states of mind.

And the riches of self-discipline, through which one may have the joy of knowing that the mind can and will serve any desired end if one will take possession and command it through definiteness of purpose.

And the riches of play, through which one may lay aside all of the burdens of life and become as a little child again.

And the riches of discovery of one's "other self"—that self which knows no such reality as permanent failure.

And the riches of FAITH IN INFINITE INTELLIGENCE, of which every individual mind is a minute projection.

And the riches of meditation, the connecting link by which any one may draw upon the great universal supply of Infinite Intelligence at will.

Yes, these and all other riches begin with a positive mental attitude. Therefore, it is but little cause for wonder that a positive mental attitude takes the first place in the list of the

"Twelve Riches."

2. SOUND PHYSICAL HEALTH

Sound health begins with a "health consciousness" produced by a mind which thinks in terms of health and not in terms of illness, plus temperance of habits in eating and properly balanced physical activities.

3. HARMONY IN HUMAN RELATIONSHIPS

Harmony with others begins with one's self, for it is true, as Shakespeare said, there are benefits available to those who comply with his admonition, "To thine own self be true, and it must follow, as the night the day, thou cans't not then be false to any man."

4. FREEDOM FROM FEAR

No man who fears anything is a free man! Fear is a harbinger of evil, and wherever it appears one may find a cause which must be eliminated before he may become rich in the fuller sense. The seven basic fears which appear most often in the minds of men are (i) the fear of POVERTY, (ii) the fear of CRITICISM, (iii) the fear of ILL HEALTH, (iv) the fear of LOSS OF LOVE, (v) the fear of the LOSS OF LIBERTY, (vi) the fear of OLD AGE, (vii) the fear of DEATH.

5. THE HOPE OF ACHIEVEMENT

The greatest of all forms of happiness comes as the result of hope of achievement of some yet unattained desire; and poor beyond description is the person who cannot look to the future with hope that he will become the person he would like to be, or with the belief that he will attain the objective he has failed to reach in the past.

6. THE CAPACITY FOR FAITH

Faith is the connecting link between the conscious mind of man and the great universal reservoir of Infinite Intelligence. It is the fertile soil of the garden of the human mind wherein may be produced all of the riches of life. It is the "eternal elixir" which gives creative power and action to the impulses of thought.

Faith is the basis of all so-called miracles, and of many mysteries which cannot be explained by the rules of logic or science.

Faith is the spiritual "chemical" which, when it is mixed with prayer, gives one direct and immediate connection with Infinite Intelligence.

Faith is the power which transmutes the ordinary energies of thought into their spiritual equivalent. And it is the only power through which the Cosmic Force of Infinite Intelligence may be appropriated to the uses of man.

7. WILLINGNESS TO SHARE ONE'S BLESSINGS

He who has not learned the blessed art of sharing has not learned the true path to happiness, for happiness comes only by sharing. And let it be forever remembered that all riches may be embellished and multiplied by the simple process of sharing them where they may serve others. And let it be also remembered that the space one occupies in the hearts of his fellowmen is determined precisely by the service he renders through some form of sharing his blessings.

Riches which are not shared, whether they be material riches or the intangibles, wither and die like the rose on a severed stem, for it is one of Nature's first laws that inaction and disuse lead to decay and death, and this law applies to the material possessions of men just as it applies to the living cells of every physical body.

8. A LABOR OF LOVE

There can be no richer man than he who has found a labor of love and who is busily engaged in performing it, for labor is the highest form of human expression of desire. Labor is the liaison between the demand and the supply of all human needs, the forerunner of all human progress, the medium by which the imagination of man is given the wings of action. And all labor of love is sanctified because it brings the joy of self-expression to him who performs it.

9. AN OPEN MIND ON ALL SUBJECTS

Tolerance, which is among the higher attributes of culture, is expressed only by the person who holds an open mind on all subjects at all times. And it is only the man with an open mind who becomes truly educated and who is thus prepared to avail himself of the greater riches of life.

10. SELF-DISCIPLINE

The man who is not the master of himself may never become the master of anything. He who is the master of self may become the master of his own earthly destiny, the "master of his fate, the Captain of his soul." And the highest form of self-discipline consists in the expression of humility of the heart when one has attained great riches or has been overtaken by that which is commonly called "success".

11. THE CAPACITY TO UNDERSTAND PEOPLE

The man who is rich in the understanding of people always recognizes that all people are fundamentally alike in that they have evolved from the same stem; that all human activities are inspired by one or more of the nine basic motives of life, viz:

1. The emotion of LOVE
2. The emotion of SEX
3. The desire for MATERIAL GAIN
4. The desire for SELF-PRESERVATION
5. The desire for FREEDOM OF BODY AND MIND
6. The desire for SELF-EXPRESSION
7. The desire for perpetuation of LIFE AFTER DEATH
8. The emotion of ANGER
9. The emotion of FEAR

And the man who would understand others must first understand himself.

The capacity to understand others eliminates many of the common causes of friction among men. It is the foundation of all friendship. It is the basis of all harmony and cooperation among men. It is the fundamental of major importance in all leadership which calls for friendly cooperation. And some believe that it is an approach of major importance to the understanding of the Creator of all things.

12. ECONOMIC SECURITY

The last, though not least in importance, is the tangible portion of the "Twelve Riches".

Economic security is not attained by the possession of money alone. It is attained by the service one renders, for useful service may be converted into all forms of human needs, with or without the use of money.

Henry Ford has economic security, not because he controls a vast fortune of money, but for the better reason that he provides profitable employment for millions of men and women, and also dependable transportation by automobile for still greater numbers of people. The service he renders has attracted the money he controls, and it is in this manner that all enduring economic security must be attained.

Presently I shall acquaint you with the principles by which money and all other forms of riches may be obtained, but first you must be prepared to make application of these principles. Your mind must be conditioned for the acceptance of riches just as the soil of the earth must be prepared for the planting of seeds.

When one is ready for a thing it is sure to appear!

This does not mean that the things one may need will appear without a cause, for there is a vast difference between one's "*needs*" and one's *readiness* to receive. To miss this distinction is to miss the major benefits which I shall endeavor to convey. So be patient and let me lead you into *readiness* to receive the riches which you desire. I shall have to lead *my way!*

BE PATIENT AND SEE THE RESULTS

My way will seem strange to you at first, but you should not become discouraged on this account, for all new ideas seem strange. If you doubt that my way is practical take courage from the fact that it has brought me riches in abundance.

Human progress always has been slow because people are reluctant to accept new ideas.

When Samuel Morse announced his system for communication by telegraph the world scoffed at him. His system was unorthodox. It was new, therefore it was subject to suspicion and doubt.

And the world scoffed at Marconi when he announced the perfection of an improvement over Morse's system; a system of communication by wireless.

Thomas A. Edison came in for ridicule when he announced his perfection of the incandescent electric light bulb, and Henry Ford met with the same experience when he offered the world a self-propelled vehicle to take the place of the horse and buggy.

When Wilbur and Orville Wright announced the perfection of a practical flying machine the world was so little impressed that the newspaper men refused to witness a demonstration of the machine.

Then came the discovery of the modern radio, one of the "miracles" of human ingenuity which was destined to make the whole world a-kin. The "unprepared" minds accepted it as a toy to amuse children but nothing more.

I mention these facts as a reminder to you, who are seeking riches by a new way, that you be not discouraged because of the newness of the way. Follow through with me, appropriate my philosophy and be assured that it will work for you as it has worked for me.

By serving as your guide to riches I shall receive my compensation for my efforts in exact proportion to the benefits you receive. The eternal law of compensation insures this. My compensation may not come directly from you who appropriate my philosophy, but come it will in one form or another, for it is a part of the great Cosmic Plan that no useful service shall be rendered by anyone without a just compensation. "Do the thing," said Emerson, "and you shall have the power."

Aside from the consideration of what I shall receive for my endeavor to serve you, there is the question of an obligation which I owe the world in return for the blessings it has bestowed upon me. I did not acquire my riches without the aid of many others. I have observed that all who acquire enduring riches have ascended the ladder of opulence with two outstretched hands; one extended upward to receive the help of others who have reached the peak, and the other extended downward to aid those who are still climbing.

And here let me admonish you who are on the path to riches that you too must proceed with outstretched hands, to give and to receive aid, for it is a well known fact that no man may attain enduring success or acquire enduring riches without aiding others who are seeking these desirable ends. To GET one must first GIVE!

I have brought this message in order that I may GIVE!

And now that we know what are the real riches of life I shall reveal to you the next step which you must take in the process of "conditioning" your mind to receive riches.

I have acknowledged that my riches came through the aid of others.

Some of these have been men well known to all who will hear my story. The men who have served as leaders in preparing the way for the rest of us, under that which we call "*The American way of life*."

Some have been strangers whose names you will not recognize.

Among these *strangers* are eight of my friends who have

done most for me in preparing my mind for the acceptance of riches. I call them the "Eight Princes." They serve me when I am awake and they serve me while I sleep.

Although I have never met the "princes" face to face, as I have met the others who have aided me, they have stood watch over my riches; they have protected me against fear and envy and greed and doubt and indecision and procrastination. They have inspired me to move on my own personal initiative, have kept my imagination active, and have given me definiteness of purpose and the faith to insure its fulfillment.

They have been the real "conditioners" of my mind, the builders of my *positive mental attitude!*

POINTS TO REMEMBER

1. All riches begin with a state of mind.
2. Find harmony in human relationships.
3. The man who is not the master of himself may never become the master of anything.

2

THE MASTER MIND GROUP—A POWER BEYOND SCIENCE

The great achievements of your life—first built as mind-concepts, then made real—are not limited to the power of your own mind. A myriad of other minds can tune in upon yours and give you their thoughts through ethereal vibration. Forming a Master Mind group is a good way to begin the process of tuning in, and when you form your group you will know you are using a technique which has mightily proved its benefit among many well-known men. All great achievements are the result of a multiplicity of minds working together harmoniously.

Was Henry Ford ignorant?

Rather than attempt to form your answer, which must come from within yourself, I shall tell you of an experience the founder of Ford Motor Company had in a courtroom. The experience really included everybody in that courtroom and a good many outside the courtroom as well.

As we know, Mr. Ford had little formal schooling. Perhaps because of this fact, the Chicago Tribune, which took exception to some of his views on war, called him an ignoramus. Mr. Ford brought suit, charging the newspaper with libel.

When the attorneys for the Tribune had Mr. Ford on the

witness stand they cross-examined him in an attempt to prove their statement was true.

One question they asked was: "How many soldiers did the British send over to subdue the rebellion in the colonies in

With a dry grin, Ford replied: "I don't know just how many, but I have heard it was a lot more than ever went back."

There was laughter from the court, the jury, the spectators, and even from the frustrated lawyer who had asked the question.

Ford kept calm through an hour or more of similar questioning on "schoolbook" topics. At length, in reply to a question which was particularly obnoxious to him, the industrialist let off some steam. He observed that he had a row of electric push-buttons hanging over his desk, and that when he wanted a question answered, he placed his finger on the right button and called in the right man to answer that question. He wanted to know why he should burden his mind with a lot of useless details when he had able men around him who could supply him with all the information he needed.

This trial occurred many years ago and I dare say that only a minority of my readers recall how it came out. If you do not know, exercise your own power to develop information by going to the library and finding out. I will say, however, that Mr. Ford's remarks resounded through that silenced courtroom, through the nation and around the world. Surely Ford's friend Thomas Edison appreciated them, for he was another who had surrounded himself with able men through whom he vastly extended his own abilities and his own mind-power, school education or no.

Thomas Paine, whose keen mind helped both in drawing up the Declaration of Independence and in persuading its signers to translate their concept into reality, spoke in memorable terms of the great storehouse of knowledge which waits to be transferred to our own storehouse. I quote him in part:

> Any person, who has made observations on the ... human mind, by observing his own, cannot but have observed that there are two classes of what are called Thoughts: those that we produce in ourselves by reflection and the act of thinking, and those that bolt into the mind of their own accord. I have always made it a rule to treat these voluntary visitors with civility, and it is from them that I have acquired almost all the knowledge that I have. As to the learning that any person gains from school education, it serves only like a small capital, to put him in the way of beginning learning for himself afterwards. Every person of learning is finally his own teacher.

Whence come the thoughts which do not originate within our own minds, out of our own experience? Often it is apparent that such thoughts are suggested by other persons in words or in writing, and later they "play back" from within our subconscious memories; or they may be a completely conscious process, as when we sit in conference with another.

All of us, however, receive thoughts which are silently broadcast by other minds and received by our own. This too is a "planted" idea we touched upon previously and now shall examine in more detail.

YOU ARE THE MASTER, YOU ARE THE MIND

What is the Master Mind? I visualize the Master Mind as a formless, boundless reservoir of thought-vibration. Not all of it can be available to any one person at any one time. When you are in harmony with another person or with a number of other people, however, the attunement of mind to mind results in a "tuning in" of incalculable value. A man who has a corps of assistants with whom he maintains amiable relations has at his disposal far more than the knowledge his assistants may give him by obvious means. Their minds constantly feed his through mental broadcast power, and receive information from his mind as well. The same is true when friends or business associates form a Master Mind group at which they discuss various topics or problems. Their several minds focused on the topic obviously add great power to the mind most occupied with it; but also an exchange of broadcast thoughts is effected right then, and also later, when the persons involved may be far apart. This is not obvious as is speech or writing, but its power goes beyond anything science can completely explain.

I have been greatly interested in observing how the science of this atomic age gives "faith and credit" in this direction to the science of fifty years ago. At that time we could list eighty-odd forms of physical matter (we list many more now) and we knew that matter is made of incredibly tiny particles with of Mind space between. We had begun to know there is so much space within matter that, in a sense, nothing is "solid." You and I, the desk at which I write, my typewriter, this dot (.) are made of atoms; the atom in turn contains electrons which either revolve in orbits or vibrate rapidly to and fro. Other particles such as neutrons are now postulated, but the principle remains the same. Whether you observe the largest star that glitters in the sky or the smallest grain of sand among billions on a beach, it is a collection of particles, space and electric charges.

Fifty years ago we had begun to have some proof that even the most minute particles are not "things" but bundles of vibrations. We knew, too, that various forms of energy proceed through air and space in their characteristic forms because of their varying frequency of vibration. Thus, vibrations beginning at about 15 per second and going up to about 15,000 per second are perceptible to the human ear as sound. Above that we no longer hear vibrations; but at around 1,500,000 vibrations per second that form of energy called heat begins and we can feel it with another of our senses.

Higher up the scale of vibration comes light, often combined with heat, and our eyes perceive this. The lowest light vibrations begin with deep red, the highest are violet, with all other colors in between. Above the vibrations of violet—some 3,000,000 per second—lie ultraviolet and other vibrations invisible to the eye but detectable by instruments.

Still higher up the scale—we cannot yet say how high—may lie the vibrations of thought, and these are the invisible, inaudible vibrations which flash from mind to mind.

Dr. Alexander Graham Bell, whose name we justly associate with the telephone, was an authority on vibration. He noted that we have no ordinary sense that can appreciate the effect of any vibration between heat and light. He said: there must be a great deal to be learned about the effect of those vibrations in the great gap where the ordinary human senses are unable to hear, see or feel the movement. The power to send wireless messages by ether vibrations lies in that gap, but the gap is so great that it seems there must be much more It seems to me that in this gap lie the vibrations which we have assumed to be given off by our brains and nerve cells when we think. But then, again, they may be higher up, in the scale beyond the vibrations that produce the ultraviolet rays [my own theory].

"It would be possible to cite many reasons why thought and vital force may be regarded as of the same nature as electricity... We may assume that the brain cells act as a battery and that the current produced flows along the nerves. But does it end there? Does it not pass out of the body in waves which flow around the world unperceived by our senses, just as the wireless waves passed unperceived before Hertz and others discovered their existence?"

Field theory and thought-transference. Einstein showed mathematically that vast fields of force pervade the universe. A field of force comes out of every wire that carries current— or we would have no electric motors, no radio or television and would lack quite a few other conveniences. Why should not a field of force emanate from the electricity which constantly passes to and fro along the conducting nerves and cells of the body? Why should they not go around the world, into space, on forever?

Now our world is both threatened and uplifted by the physical realization of Einstein's great mind-concept of nearly sixty years ago: $E=mc^2$. This formula governs the conversion of mass into energy, and accounts for the enormous energy put to use in atomic power plants and the atomic bomb. In using atomic power we prove once and for all, for everyone to see, that mass is energy. Since energy is vibration, everything undoubtedly is vibration. You and I now know we are vibration—beyond the shadow of a doubt.

STEPS TO BENEFIT FROM THE MASTER MIND PRINCIPLE

Tune your radio to the known vibration-rate of any radio station as indicated on the tuning dial, and you sensitize your radio to that particular vibration; the radio then changes it into vibrations you can hear. Is there anything strange about a natural "tuning" to the omnipresent thought-vibrations of another mind which already has shown its empathy with your own mind? It is no more strange than radio. Radio's laws at length were discovered. So shall the laws of thought-broadcast and reception some day be discovered, and the natural apparatus we now use but dimly shall be at everyone's command.

You understand now that whenever two or more minds are blended in a spirit of perfect harmony, for the pursuit of a definite purpose, there is born of that alliance a power which is greater than that of all the individual minds combined.

This is the Master Mind principle. It does not interfere with your possession of yourself. In fact, one who is himself in all ways is all the more able to accept ideas from the minds of others peacefully and usefully, since he is in no danger of being overwhelmed. The Science of Personal Achievement was born out of a Master Mind alliance, my allies having been those five hundred and more successful men whom I interviewed and worked with in the course of many years.

A person who has peace of mind always gives as well as receives. As you apply the Master Mind principle, you not only share your knowledge with others but also place yourself in a position to receive generously from others—and that which you receive can multiply your power to grow rich far beyond your present conception.

Here, then, are the steps to take in order to avail yourself of the boundless benefits of the Master Mind principle:

1. **Your Master Mind round table.** Begin by inviting two or three people whom you know well to join you in your undertaking. Be sure that these people are in harmony with you and with one another. Explain that the major purpose of the alliance is mutual growth mentally and spiritually, while you certainly will accept the material benefits which naturally attend such development.

2. **You are not a debating society.** Make it clear from the beginning that such controversial matters as politics, religion and similarly touchy topics have no place in your group meetings. Your aim is to aid one another with knowledge based on the experience each member has gained from life.
3. **Your discussion is confidential.** Discussion and cooperation must stay within the group. Knowing this, all will be encouraged to speak freely.
4. **The group will be allowed to grow.** From time to time, the group may be enlarged by additional members. It should not be allowed to grow so large as to become unwieldy. Any new member must be subject to a unanimous vote of acceptance.
5. **Provide for a trial election.** With the exception of the original members of the Master Mind group, members may be elected for one month or for some other convenient period. You should be perfectly frank about the necessity of making sure that any new member is in harmony with the others, and that if you ask him to leave the group it is no reflection upon his personal worth.
6. **Agree on general principles of life-success.** Bear in mind that if any one of your round-table members does not believe, for instance, that he should give completely of his knowledge and experience, he will create disharmony and you may get nowhere. I suggest that you all agree on the principles set forth in this book.
7. **Rotate your chairmen and your "board of directors".** Each person should serve in turn as the chairman. He should see that all members take part in the discussion; that questions are asked freely and personal experiences

freely described. He should ask each speaker to stand as he speaks, to help him develop poise while speaking "on his feet." He should enforce any time limit agreed upon, so as to prevent the more verbose members from consuming more than their share of the time. Rotation of the chairmen will automatically result in the rotation of members of the "board" who listen to the speaker, who thus wins a variety of minds to serve him.

8. **When a group consists of fellow-workers.** When a Master Mind group consists of the employees of a single business, it should contain members of management as well as members of the rank-and-file. This plan has been followed with a great development of friendly co-operation, benefit to the business as well as benefit to the individuals concerned.

9. **Adopt a major purpose.** In addition to the individual purposes and problems which will be aired, the group as a whole should adopt some major purpose or project, to be carried on jointly by all its members for the benefit of people who are not in the group. One such project was that of conducting a Personal Problem Clinic once a week, at which the public was invited to bring in personal problems for consideration by the group, sitting as a Personal Problem Court. When a project is completed, another should be chosen.

TAKE THE LEAD

Since part of this book's purpose is to spare you from learning by trial and error, I shall set down some lessons already learned that way—by myself and others.

I suggest that you do not reveal the private purposes of your

Master Mind alliance to those outside the group. Remember the many who are wedded to failure and who channel their efforts—not toward success—but toward trying to tear down others. Such persons will scoff at the Master Mind principle. Their scoffing need not annoy you, but it may; and at any rate, you need nobody's opinion but your own so far as forming your group is concerned.

When you sit down with your Master Mind group, make sure you leave all negative points of view behind. Your meetings should be your greatest signal to find and hold a positive mental attitude. Moreover, as leader of your Master Mind group it is your duty to show your own enthusiasm and allow others to share this valuable emotion. (Don't worry about the mechanics of sharing your enthusiasm, for there is no other emotion that is so "catching"!)

Take care to see that every member of the group receives something out of every meeting. Enthusiasm and co-operation will grow in proportion to the rewards every man bears away with him.

A Master Mind group is not a place in which to bring competitors together. Nobody in the group should have reason to feel antagonistic toward any other member, nor have any motive for keeping secrets from him. Remember that confidence is the basis of all harmonious relationships. Form your group out of people in whom you have confidence; make sure they have confidence in you.

Millions of people need a Personal Problem Clinic. I purposefully repeat that every Master Mind should have a group purpose which benefits those outside the group. This principle is so important that I shall enlarge upon the idea of the Personal Problem Clinic, surely one of the best public services any group can perform.

Let us look at a number of typical applications.

If I were a life insurance agent, I would conduct such a clinic twice weekly, if possible. The modern life insurance man is looked upon as a counselor in several fields of family concern, budget for example. While giving of your time and telling your own life-experience and that of others, you may well form an indelible impression upon men and women who need life insurance.

If I were a clergyman, I would conduct a Personal Problem Clinic going far beyond the members of my own congregation. I would have sitting with me, as Board of Counselors, the ablest members of my church, representing a wide variety of businesses and professions. I would expect no direct reward, but would be gratified if my services helped to fill the pews of my church every Sunday.

If I were a schoolteacher, I would recognize that parents who are led to a harmonious solution of their problems are better parents, better able to help their children. I would conduct a clinic in the hopes that both generations would benefit and that the benefit would be reflected in the ability of my pupils to retain what I teach and grow into better citizens.

If I were a physician, dentist, osteopath, chiropractor or naturopath, I would conduct a clinic for the benefit of my patients and I would invite them to bring their friends and neighbors with them. Knowing that much illness originates in the mind, I would take this opportunity to heal where I could and in other cases to speed the processes of healing.

If I were the head of a family that included growing children, I would conduct a Personal Problem Clinic for each member of the family. I might very well invite my neighbors to join.

I have pointed out some of the benefits which may accrue

to you from running a Personal Problem Clinic. You may see no benefit; but rest assured that any benefit you send out into the world will come back to you in some way, at some time, perhaps a thousand times multiplied.

The late Mahatma Gandhi made himself one of the greatest benefactors of all time by the simple process of serving his countrymen without limit and without thought of financial reward. He was probably in the hearts of more men than any other man who ever lived. He drew several hundred million of his Indian countrymen to him of their own free will, and his reward—the independence of his nation—was a reward greater than most of us ever dream of achieving.

Your Master Mind group of necessity will be a small group. Yet when you extend it out into the world through a Personal Problem Clinic—through adopting the sponsorship of a Boys' Club or some other welfare agency—or whatever other group project you may choose, your mind will automatically feel the effect of many other minds in harmony with your purpose. Here are illimitable riches!

GIVE AND BE HUMBLE!

The Master Mind principle in politics. In speaking with some men who hold political office, I have been saddened momentarily by what they call their "hard-headed" attitude. Once they are voted into power they tend to wield that power like a club, arbitrarily swinging their influence with little regard to those who must obey the rules they set. This is not so with the truly great men; but unfortunately, a good many small-minded men achieve public office.

If I were the mayor of a town or city, I would set up a People's Personal Problem Clinic in the City Hall. The counsellors in the Clinic would be the keenest minds in the city—lawyers, doctors, teachers, bankers, builders—a cross-section of such a variety of human talent that any citizen could rely upon finding an understanding ear.

I would hold clinic sessions at some stated hour at least once a week. As the clinic attracted more and more people, I might find it advisable to organize it into subgroups. I certainly would arrange for private counsel to be available in emergencies between meetings, and to follow up on particular cases if need be.

My reward? I believe that any mayor who did this would maintain himself in office for as long as he wished. Yet this is only a secondary reward. The real reward would lie in knowing that I have lifted government to a new, high plane of individuality and humanity.

Your mind is strengthened by peace and harmony. Do you expect your life to bring you only harmony and peace? Life indeed would be dull if it did not have its times of conflict, of problems to be solved. We grow as we overcome difficulties. If the solving of problems were not so important a part of the learning process, we would learn few of the lessons of life.

When peace and harmony remain as the veritable foundation-stones of thought and emotion, however, problems are solved with a strength which truly "passeth understanding."

Even temporary peace is a great sustaining force. Doctors often recommend a change of climate for certain types of patients. The climate itself may or may not have something to do with the healing process; more important is the change of scene. New faces, new landscapes bring the mind away from its accustomed squirrel cage of worries. "Miracle" cures have been effected when a patient walked out peacefully among the trees and the hills.

As you become better and better acquainted with your own mind, you will find it possible to hold harmony within your mind no matter what goes on around you. Meanwhile, try consciously at some time of the day to attune your mind to peace, not conflict—rest, not striving.

After a while, as you sit or walk or lie quietly alone, you may feel as though harmony is flowing into your mind from sources outside. Indeed this is true, for it is possible for any harmonious mind to tune in to yours when you have made your mind receptive.

THE IMPORTANCE OF HARMONY IN YOUR HOME

Now you can see that when I have spoken of harmony in your home I have spoken of more than a merely pleasant situation. Harmony in the home is a pervasive force which flows continually in and out of the mind-circuits and conditions the mind to keep itself in peace and continued harmony.

We live in a home where harmony and affection are the dominating spirits. Everything we do in our home gives us pleasure, including our work, which is a work of love.

Now and again, my wife and I take a long walk, or perhaps a drive into the country. We return refreshed with thoughts of new faces, new scenes, perhaps new experiences—and glad to return to a home that is good to come back to.

Find your own way to get rid of worry—but keep it simple. In II Kings, Chapter Five, you may read the story of Naaman, captain of the host of the King of Syria. This rich and powerful man was afflicted with leprosy. He called upon the prophet Elisha to cure him, expecting Elisha to come up with some complicated and mysterious rigmarole. But Elisha merely said: "Go and wash in Jordan seven times and thy flesh shall come again to thee, and thou shalt be clean."

Perhaps this story is a parable, showing us that there generally is a simple way out of our troubles. I do not deny the existence of very serious troubles; but I have noticed that the great majority of troubles are minor annoyances which lead to a pattern of annoyance and worry. Feed your mind on little worries and it will develop quite an appetite for big worries.

The greatest buttress of worry is—sitting around and thinking about your worry. This adds strength to the worry, which thereupon sends stronger and stronger roots into the mind which nourishes it.

The greatest destroyer and uprooter of worry is—transmuting the worry-reaction into some sort of constructive activity. By going into action, make your mind focus on that action. By using your muscles, however mildly, you give a rest to your mind.

I have a friend who has a novel way of dealing with worries. He goes out into his garden and hoes vigorously until he has worked up a good perspiration.

Others, perhaps not so vigorous, may cancel worry by attending to some bit of craftsmanship or carpentry. And then, of course, there is the excellent procedure of turning your mind toward helping someone else solve his problem, a method available even to the bedridden.

But nothing complicated! In this book we talk of many things, and you would do well to come back to this section now and then to refresh yourself with the idea that peace of mind is essentially a simple state of being. It is often remarked that some successful, highly placed men are really "quite simple fellows" when you get to know them. Indeed they are—no matter of how high an order may be their intelligence. An efficient mind attains a basic simplicity upon which all else is built.

I am reminded of a man who was greatly benefited by participating in a Master Mind alliance. He said that his greatest benefit came from being helped to see his problems through others' eyes and thus to see, at last, how simple his problems were. He said he had been in the habit of multiplying his problems by each other and looking at the sum, which was tremendous. When he took his problems one by one they were quickly solved, and his mind began clicking as it never had before.

The Supreme Secret is as inherent in this chapter as a book is inherent in the mind that conceives its plan.

POINTS TO REMEMBER

1. All great achievements are the result of a multiplicity of minds working together harmoniously.
2. Don't burden your mind with useless details.
3. A person who has peace of mind always gives as well as receives.

3

INITIATIVE AND LEADERSHIP

Initiative and Leadership are associated terms in this lesson for the reason that *leadership* is essential for the attainment of *Success*, and *Initiative* is the very foundation upon which this necessary quality of *leadership* is built. *Initiative* is as essential to success as a hub is essential to a wagon wheel.

And what is *Initiative?*

It is that exceedingly rare quality that prompts—nay, impels—a person to do that which ought to be done *without being told to do it.* Elbert Hubbard expressed himself on the subject of *initiative* in the words:

"The world bestows its big prizes, both in money and honors, for one thing, and that is *Initiative.*

"What is initiative? I'll tell you: It is doing the right thing without being told.

"But next to doing the right thing without being told is to do it when you are told once. That is to say, 'Carry the message to Garcia.' Those who can carry a message get high honors, but their pay is not always in proportion.

"Next, there are those who do the right thing when necessity kicks them from behind, and these get indifference instead of honors, and a pittance for pay.

"This kind spend most of the time polishing a bench with

a hard luck story.

"Then, still lower down in the scale than this we have the fellow who will not do the right thing even when someone goes along to show him how and stays to see that he does it; he is always out of a job, a receives the contempt he deserves, unless he has a rich pa, in which case destiny patiently waits around the corner with a stuffed club.

"To which class do *you* belong?"

Inasmuch as you will be expected to take inventory of yourself and determine which factors of this course you need most, after you have completed it, it may be well if you begin to get ready for this analysis by answering the question that Elbert Hubbard has asked:

To which class do you belong?

One of the peculiarities of L*eadership* is the fact that it is never found in those who have not acquired the *habit* of taking the initiative. *Leadership* is something that you must invite yourself into; it will never thrust itself upon you. If you will carefully analyze all leaders whom you know you will see that they not only exercised *Initiative*, but they went about their work with a *definite purpose* in mind. You will also see that they possessed the quality of *Self-confidence.*

These facts are mentioned in this lesson for the reason that it will profit you to observe that successful people make use of all the factors covered by the lessons of the course; and, for the more important reason that it will profit you to understand thoroughly the principle of *organized effort* which this Reading Course is intended to establish in your mind.

This seems an appropriate place to state that this course is not intended as a *shortcut* to success, nor is it intended as a mechanical formula that you may use in noteworthy achievement without effort on your part. The *real* value of the course lies in the *use* that you will make of it, and not in the course itself. The chief purpose of the course is to help you develop in yourself the qualities covered by the lessons of the course, and one of the most important of these qualities is *Initiative*, the subject of this lesson.

We will now proceed to apply the principle upon which this lesson is founded by describing, in detail, just how it served successfully to complete a business transaction which most people would call difficult.

In 1916 I needed $25,000.00 with which to create an educational institution, but I had neither this sum nor sufficient collateral with which to borrow it through the usual banking sources. Did I bemoan my fate or think of what I might accomplish if some rich relative or Good Samaritan would come to my rescue by loaning me the necessary capital?

I did nothing of the sort!

I did just what you will be advised, throughout this course, to do. First of all, I made the securing of this capital my *definite chief aim*. Second, I laid out a complete *plan* through which to transform this aim into reality. Backed by sufficient Self-confidence and spurred on by *Initiative*, I proceeded to put my plan into action. But, before the "action" stage of the plan had been reached, more than six weeks of constant, persistent study and effort and thought were embodied in it. If a plan is to be sound it must be built of carefully chosen material.

HOW TO BE AN INITIATOR

There are generally many plans through the operation of which a desired object may be achieved, and it often happens to be true that the obvious and usual methods employed are not the best. The usual method of procedure, in the case related, would have been that of borrowing from a bank. You can see that this method was impractical, in this case, for the reason that no collateral was available.

A great philosopher once said: *"Initiative is the pass-key that opens the door to opportunity"*.

I do not recall who this philosopher was, but I know that he was *great* because of the soundness of his statement.

We will now proceed to outline the exact procedure that you must follow if you are to become a person of *initiative* and *leadership*.

First: You must master the habit of *procrastination* and eliminate it from your make-up. This habit of putting off until tomorrow that which you should have done last week or last year or a score of years ago is gnawing at the very vitals of your being, and you can accomplish nothing until you throw it off.

The method through which you eliminate *procrastination* is based upon a well known and scientifically tested principle of psychology which has been referred to in the two preceding lessons of this course as Autosuggestion.

Copy the following formula and place it conspicuously in your room where you will see it as you retire at night and as you arise in the morning:

INITIATIVE AND LEADERSHIP

I realize that the place to begin developing the *habit of initiative* is in the small, commonplace things connected with my daily work, therefore I will go at my work each day as if I were doing it solely for the purpose of developing this necessary *habit of initiative*.

I understand that by practicing this *habit of* taking the *initiative* in connection with my daily work I will be not only developing that habit, but I will also be attracting the attention of those who will place greater value on my services as a result of this practice.

Signed ....

Regardless of what you are now doing, every day brings you face to face with a chance to render some service, outside of the course of your regular duties, that will be of value to others. In rendering this additional service, of your own accord, you of course understand that you are not doing so with the object of receiving monetary pay. You are rendering this service because it provides you with ways and means of exercising, developing and making stronger the aggressive spirit of *initiative* which you must possess before you can ever become an outstanding figure in the affairs of your chosen field of life-work.

Those who work for *money* alone, and who receive for their pay nothing but money, are always underpaid, no matter how much they receive. Money is necessary, but the big prizes of life cannot be measured in dollars and cents.

No amount of money could possibly be made to take the place of the happiness and joy and pride that belong to the person who digs a better ditch, or builds a better chicken coop, or sweeps a cleaner floor, or cooks a better meal. Every normal person loves to create something that is better than the average. The joy of *creating* a work of art is a joy that cannot be replaced by money or any other form of material possession.

The brand of *leadership* that is recommended through this course of instruction is the brand which leads to self-determination and freedom and self-development and enlightenment and justice. This is the brand that endures. For example, and as a contrast with the brand of *leadership* through which Napoleon raised himself into prominence, consider our own American commoner, Lincoln. The object of his *leadership* was to bring truth and justice and understanding to the people of the United States. Even though he died a martyr to his belief in this brand of *leadership*, his name has been engraved upon the heart of the world in terms of loving kindliness that will never bring aught but good to the world.

POINTS TO REMEMBER

1. No one could become an efficient leader without belief in himself.
2. *Initiative* is the very foundation upon which this necessary quality of *leadership* is built.
3. Money is necessary, but the big prizes of life cannot be measured in dollars and cents.

4

ACCURATE THOUGHT

This is at one and the same time the most *important*, the most *interesting* and the most difficult to present lesson of this entire course.

It is important because it deals with a principle which runs through the entire course. It is interesting for the same reason. It is difficult to present for the reason that it will carry the average student far beyond the boundary line of his common experiences and into a realm of *thought* in which he is not accustomed to dwell.

Unless you study this lesson with an open mind, you will miss the very keystone to the arch of this course, and without this stone you can never complete your Temple of Success.

This lesson will bring you a conception of *thought* which may carry you far above the level to which you have risen by the evolutionary processes to which you have been subjected in the past; and, for this reason, you should not be disappointed if, at first reading, you do not fully understand it. Most of us *disbelieve* that which we cannot understand, and it is with knowledge of this human tendency in mind that I caution you against closing your mind if you do not grasp all that is in this lesson at the first reading.

For thousands of years men made ships of wood, and of

nothing else. They used wood because they believed that it was the only substance that would float; but that was because they had not yet advanced far enough in their *thinking* process to understand the truth that steel will float, and that it is far superior to wood for the building of ships. They did not know that anything could float which was lighter than the amount of water is displaced, and until they learned of this great truth they went on making ships of wood.

Until some twenty-five years ago, most men thought that only the birds could fly, but now we know that man can not only equal the flying of the birds, but he can excel it.

Men did not know, until quite recently, that the great open void known as the air is more alive and more sensitive than anything that is on the earth. They did not know that the spoken word would travel through the ether with the speed of a flash of lightning, without the aid of wires. How could they know this when their minds had not been unfolded sufficiently to enable them to grasp it? The purpose of this lesson is to aid *you* in so unfolding and expanding your mind that you will be able to *think* with accuracy, for this unfoldment will open to you a door that leads to all the power you will need in completing your Temple of Success.

All through the preceding lessons of this course you observed that we have dealt with principles which any one could easily grasp and apply. You will also observe that these principles have been so presented that they lead to *success* as measured by material wealth. This seemed necessary for the reason that to most people the word *success* and the word *money* are synonymous terms. Obviously, the previous lessons of this course were intended for those who look upon worldly things and material wealth as being all that there is to *success*.

Presenting the matter in another way, I was conscious of

the fact that the majority of the students of this course would feel disappointed if I pointed out to them a roadway to *success* that leads through other than the doorways of business, and finance, and industry; for it is a matter of common knowledge that most men want success that is spelled SUCCESS!

Very well—let those who are satisfied with this standard of *success* have it; but some there are who will want to go higher up the ladder, in search of *success* which is measured in other than material standards, and it is for their benefit in particular that this and the subsequent lessons of this course are intended.

◆

Accurate thought involves two fundamentals which all who indulge in it must observe. First, to think accurately you must separate *facts* from mere *information*. There is much "information" available to you that is not based upon facts. Second, you must separate *facts* into two classes; namely, the *important* and the *unimportant*, or, the *relevant* and the *irrelevant*.

Only by so doing can you think clearly.

All *facts* which you can use in the attainment of your *definite chief aim* are important and relevant; all that you cannot use are unimportant and irrelevant. It is mainly the neglect of some to make this distinction which accounts for the chasm which separates so widely people who appear to have equal ability, and who have had equal opportunity. Without going outside of your own circle of acquaintances you can point to one or more persons who have had no greater opportunity than you have had, and who appear to have no more, and perhaps less, ability than you, who are achieving far greater success.

And you wonder why!

Search diligently and you will discover that all such people have acquired the habit of combining and using the *important facts* which affect their line of work. Far from working harder than you, they are perhaps working less and with greater ease. By virtue of their having learned the secret of separating the *important facts* from the *unimportant,* they have provided themselves with a sort of fulcrum and lever with which they can move with their little fingers loads that you cannot budge with the entire weight of your body.

The person who forms the habit of directing his attention to the *important facts* out of which he is constructing his Temple of Success, thereby provides himself with a power which may be likened to a trip-hammer which strikes a ten-ton blow as compared to a tack-hammer which strikes a one-pound blow!

If these similes appear to be elementary you must keep in mind the fact that some of the students of this course have not yet developed the capacity to think in more complicated terms, and to try to force them to do so would be the equivalent of leaving them hopelessly behind.

That you may understand the importance of distinguishing between *facts* and mere *information,* study that type of man who is guided entirely by that which he hears; the type who is influenced by all the "whisperings of the winds of gossip"; that accepts, without analysis, all that he reads in the newspapers and judges others by what their enemies and competitors and contemporaries say about them.

THE FACT ABOUT FACTS

Search your circle of acquaintances and pick out one of this type as an example to keep before your mind while we are on this subject. Observe that this man usually begins his conversation with some such term as this—*"I see by the papers,"* or *"they say."*

The accurate thinker knows that the newspapers are not always accurate in their reports, and he also knows that what "they say" usually carries more falsehood than truth. If you have not risen above the *"I see by the papers,"* and the *"they say"* class, you have still far to go before you become an *accurate thinker.* Of course, much truth and many *facts* travel in the guise of idle gossip and newspaper reports; but the *accurate thinker* will not accept as such all that he sees and hears.

This is a point which I feel impelled to emphasize, for the reason that it constitutes the rocks and reefs on which so many people flounder and go down to defeat in a bottomless ocean of false conclusions.

In the realm of legal procedure, there is a principle which is called the law of *evidence*; and the object of this law is to get at the *facts.* Any judge can proceed with justice to all concerned, if he has the *facts* upon which to base his judgment, but he may play havoc with innocent people if he circumvents the law of *evidence* and reaches a conclusion or judgment that is based upon *hearsay information.*

The law of Evidence varies according to the subject and circumstances with which it is used, but you will not go far wrong if, in the absence of that which you know to be *facts,* you form your judgments on the hypothesis that only that part of the evidence before you which furthers your own interests *without working any hardship on others* is based upon *facts.*

This is a crucial and *important* point in this lesson; therefore, I wish to be sure that you do not pass it by lightly. Many a man mistakes, knowingly or otherwise, expediency for *fact;* doing a thing, or refraining from doing it, for the sole reason that his action furthers his own interest without consideration as to whether it interferes with the rights of others.

No matter how regrettable, it is true that most thinking of

today, far from being *accurate,* is based upon the sole foundation of expediency. It is amazing to the more advanced student of *accurate thought,* how many people there are who are "honest" when it is profitable to them, but find myriads of facts (?) to justify themselves in following a dishonest course when that course seems to be more profitable or advantageous.

No doubt you know people who are like that.

The *accurate thinker* adopts a standard by which he guides himself, and he follows that standard at all times, whether it works always to his immediate advantage, or carries him, now and then, through the fields of disadvantage (as it undoubtedly will).

The *accurate thinker* deals with facts, regardless of how they affect his own interests, for he knows that ultimately this policy will bring him out on top, in full possession of the object of his *definite chief aim* in life. He understands the soundness of the philosophy that the old philosopher, Croesus, had in mind when he said:

"There is a wheel on which the affairs of men revolve, and its mechanism is such that it prevents any man from being *always* fortunate."

The *accurate thinker has* but one standard by which he conducts himself, in his intercourse with his fellow men, and that standard is observed by him as faithfully when it brings him temporary disadvantage as it is when it brings him outstanding advantage; for, being an *accurate thinker,* he knows that, by the law of averages, he will more than regain at some future time that which he loses by applying his standard to his own temporary detriment.

You might as well begin to prepare yourself to understand that it requires the staunchest and most unshakable *character* to become an *accurate thinker,* for you can see that this is where the reasoning of this lesson is leading.

There is a certain amount of temporary penalty attached to *accurate thinking,* there is no denying this fact; but, while this is true, it is also true that the compensating *reward,* in the aggregate, is so overwhelmingly greater that you will gladly pay this penalty.

In searching for *facts* it is often necessary to gather them through the sole source of knowledge and experience of others. It then becomes necessary to examine carefully both the evidence submitted and the person from whom the evidence comes; and when the evidence is of such a nature that it affects the interest of the witness who is giving it, there will be reason to scrutinize it all the more carefully, as witnesses who have an interest in the evidence that they are submitting often yield to the temptation to color and pervert it to protect that interest.

If one man slanders another, his remarks should be accepted, if of any weight at all, with at least a grain of the proverbial salt of caution; for it is a common human tendency for men to find nothing but evil in those whom they do not like. The man who has attained to the degree of *accurate thinking* that enables him to speak of his enemy without exaggerating his faults, and minimizing his virtues, is the exception and not the rule.

Some very able men have not yet risen above this vulgar and self-destructive habit of belittling their enemies, competitors and contemporaries. I wish to bring this common tendency to your attention with all possible emphasis, because it is a tendency that is fatal to *accurate thinking.*

Before you can become an *accurate thinker,* you must understand and make allowance for the fact that the moment a man or a woman begins to assume leadership in any walk of life, the slanderers begin to circulate "rumors" and subtle whisperings reflecting upon his or her character.

NEVER UNDERESTIMATE YOUR OPPONENT

Many a man has gone down to defeat because, due to his prejudice and hatred, he underestimated the virtues of his enemies or competitors. The eyes of the *accurate thinker* see *facts*—not the delusions of prejudice, hate and envy.

An *accurate thinker* must be something of a good sportsman—in that he is fair enough (with himself at least) to look for virtues as well as faults in other people, for it is not without reason to suppose that all men have some of each of these qualities.

"I do not believe that I can afford to deceive others—*I know I cannot afford to deceive myself!*"

This must be the motto of the *accurate thinker*.

◆

With the supposition that these "hints" are sufficient to impress upon your mind the importance of searching for *facts* until you are reasonably sure that you have found them, we will take up the question of organizing, classifying and using these *facts*.

Look, once more, in the circle of your own acquaintances and find a person who appears to accomplish more with less effort than do any of his associates. Study this man and you observe that he is a strategist in that he has learned how to arrange *facts* so that he brings to his aid the Law of Increasing Returns which we described in a previous lesson.

The man who *knows* that he is working with *facts* goes at his task with a feeling of *self-confidence* which enables him to refrain from temporizing, hesitating or waiting to make sure of his ground. He knows in advance what the outcome of his efforts will be; therefore, he moves more rapidly and accomplishes more than does the man who must "feel his way" because he is not sure that he is working with *facts*.

The man who has learned of the advantages of searching for *facts* as the foundation of his thinking has gone a very long way toward the development of *accurate thinking*, but the man who has learned how to separate *facts* into the *important* and the *unimportant* has gone still further. The latter may be compared to the man who uses a trip-hammer, and thereby accomplishes at one blow more than the former, who uses a tack-hammer, can accomplish with ten thousand blows.

To make use of *creative thought*, one must work very largely on faith, which is the chief reason why more of us do not indulge in this sort of *thought*. The most ignorant of the race can *think* in terms of deductive reasoning, in connection with matters of a purely physical and material nature, but to go a step higher and *think* in terms of *infinite intelligence* is another question. The average man is totally at sea the moment he gets beyond that which he can comprehend with the aid of his five physical senses of seeing, hearing, feeling, smelling and tasting. *Infinite intelligence* works through none of these agencies and we cannot invoke its aid through any of them.

How, then, may one appropriate the power of *infinite intelligence*? Is but a natural question. And the answer is:

Through creative thought!

THE INFINITENESS OF INTELLECT

To make clear the exact manner in which this is done I will now call your attention to some of the preceding lessons of this course through which you have been prepared to understand the meaning of *creative thought*.

In the second lesson, and to some extent in practically every other lesson that followed it, up to this one, you have observed the frequent introduction of the term "Autosuggestion." (Suggestion that you make to yourself.) We now come back to that term again, because Autosuggestion is the telegraph line, so to speak, over which you may register in your subconscious mind a description or plan of that which you wish to *create* or acquire in physical form.

It is a process you can easily learn to use.

The subconscious mind is the intermediary between the conscious *thinking* mind and *infinite intelligence*, and you can invoke the aid of *infinite intelligence* only through the medium of the subconscious mind, by giving it clear instructions as to what you want. Here you become familiar with the psychological reason for a *definite chief aim*.

If you have not already seen the importance of creating a *definite chief aim* as the object of your life-work, you will undoubtedly do so before this lesson shall have been mastered.

Knowing, from my own experience as a beginner in the study of this and related subjects, how little I understood such terms as "Subconscious Mind" and "Autosuggestion" and "*Creative Thought*," I have taken the liberty, throughout this course, of describing these terms through every conceivable simile and illustration, with the object of making their meaning and the method of their application so clear that no student of this course can possibly fail to understand. This accounts for the repetition of terms which you will observe throughout the course, and at the same time serves as an apology to those students who have already advanced far enough to grasp the meaning of much that the beginner will not understand at first reading.

The subconscious mind has one outstanding characteristic to which I will now direct your attention; namely, *it records the suggestions which you send it through Autosuggestion, and invokes the aid of infinite intelligence in translating these suggestions into their natural physical form, through natural means which are in no way out of the ordinary.* If is important that you understand the foregoing sentence, for, if you fail to understand it, you are likely to fail, also, to understand the importance of the very foundation upon which this entire course is built—*that foundation being the principle of infinite intelligence,* which may be reached and appropriated at will through aid of the law of the "Master Mind" described in the Introductory Lesson.

Study carefully, thoughtfully and with meditation, the entire preceding paragraph.

The subconscious mind has another outstanding characteristic—it accepts and acts upon all suggestions that reach it, whether they are constructive or destructive, and whether they come from the outside or from your own conscious mind.

You can see, therefore, how essential it is for you to observe the law of evidence and carefully follow the principles laid down in the beginning of this lesson, in the selection of that which you will pass on to your subconscious mind through Autosuggestion. You can see why one must search diligently for facts, and why one cannot afford to lend a receptive ear to the slanderer and the scandalmonger—for to do so is the equivalent of feeding the subconscious mind with food that is poison and ruinous to creative thought.

The sub-conscious mind may be likened to the sensitive plate of a camera on which the picture of any object placed before the camera will be recorded. The plate of the camera does not choose the sort of picture to be recorded on it, it records anything which reaches it through the lens. The conscious mind may be likened to the shutter which shuts off the light from the sensitized plate, permitting nothing to reach the plate for record except that which the operator wishes to reach it. The lens of the camera may be likened to Autosuggestion, for it is the medium which carries the image of the object to be registered, to the sensitized plate of the camera. And *infinite intelligence* may be likened to the one who develops the sensitized plate, after a picture has been recorded on it, thus bringing the picture into physical reality.

The ordinary camera is a splendid instrument with which to compare the whole process of *creative thought*. First comes the selection of the object to be exposed before the camera. This represents one's *definite chief aim* in life. Then comes the actual operation of recording a clear outline of that *purpose,* through the lens of Autosuggestion, on the sensitized plate of the subconscious mind. Here *infinite intelligence* steps in and develops the outline of that *purpose* in a physical form appropriate to the nature of the purpose. The part which *you* must play is clear!

You select the picture to be recorded (*definite chief aim).* Then you fix your conscious mind upon this purpose with such intensity that it communicates with the sub-conscious mind, through Autosuggestion, and registers that picture. You then begin to watch for and to expect manifestations of physical realization of the subject of that picture.

Bear in mind the fact that you do not sit down and wait, nor do you go to bed and sleep, with the expectation of awaking to find that *infinite intelligence* has showered you with the object of your *definite chief aim*. You go right ahead, in the usual way, doing your daily work, *with full faith and confidence that natural ways and means for the attainment of the object of your definite purpose will open to you at the proper time and in a suitable manner.*

The way may not open suddenly, from the first step to the last, but it may open one step at a time.

Therefore, when you are conscious of an opportunity to take the first step, take it without hesitation, and do the same when the second, and the third, and all subsequent steps, essential for the attainment of the object of your *definite chief aim*, are manifested to you.

POINTS TO REMEMBER

1. The two fundamentals of accurate thought.
2. It requires the staunchest and most unshakable *character* to become an *accurate thinker.*
3. There are only rumors of those who are happy and successful.

5

TOLERANCE

There are two significant features about intolerance, and your attention is directed to these at the beginning of this lesson.

These features are:

First: Intolerance is a form of ignorance which must be mastered before any form of enduring success may be attained. It is the chief cause of all wars. It makes enemies in business and in the professions. It disintegrates the organized forces of society in a thousand forms, and stands, like a mighty giant, as a barrier to the abolition of war. It dethrones reason and substitutes mob psychology in its place.

Second: Intolerance is the chief disintegrating force in the organized religions of the world, where it plays havoc with the greatest power for good there is on this earth; by breaking up that power into small sects and denominations which spend as much effort opposing each other as they do in destroying the evils of the world.

But this indictment against intolerance is general. Let's see how it affects you, the individual. It is, of course, obvious that anything which impedes the progress of civilization stands, also, as a barrier to each individual; and, stating it conversely, anything that beclouds the mind of the individual and retards his mental, moral and spiritual development, retards, also, the progress of civilization.

All of which is an abstract statement of a great truth; and, inasmuch as abstract statements am neither interesting nor highly informative, let us proceed to illustrate more concretely the damaging effects of intolerance.

I will begin this illustration by describing an incident which I have mentioned quite freely in practically every public address that I have delivered within the past five years; but, inasmuch as the cold printed page has a modifying effect which makes possible the misinterpretation of the incident here described, I believe it necessary to caution you not to read back of the lines a meaning which I had no intention of placing there. You will do yourself an injustice if you either neglect or intentionally refuse to study this illustration in the exact words and with the exact meaning which I have intended those words to convey—a meaning as clear as I know how to make the English language convey it.

As you read of this incident, place yourself in my position and see if you, also, have not had a parallel experience, and, if so, what lesson did it teach you?

One day I was introduced to a young man of unusually fine appearance. His clear eye, his warm handclasp, the tone of his voice and the splendid taste with which he was groomed marked him as a young man of the highest intellectual type. He was of the typical young American college student type, and as I ran my eyes over him, hurriedly studying his personality, as one will naturally do under such circumstances, I observed a Knights of Columbus pin on his vest.

Instantly, I released his hand as if it were a piece of ice!

This was done so quickly that it surprised both him and me. As I excused myself and started to walk away, I glanced down at the Masonic pin that I wore on my own vest, then took another look at his Knights of Columbus pin, and wondered why a couple of trinkets such as these could dig such a deep chasm between men who knew nothing of each other.

All the remainder of that day I kept thinking of the incident, because it bothered me. I had always taken considerable pride in the thought that I was tolerant with all men; but here was a spontaneous outburst of intolerance which proved that down in my sub-conscious mind existed a complex that was influencing me toward narrow-mindedness.

SELF-ANALYSIS

This discovery so shocked me that I began a systematic process of psycho-analysis through which I searched into the very depths of my soul for the cause of my rudeness.

I asked myself over and over again:

"Why did you abruptly release that young man's hand and turn away from him, when you knew nothing about him?"

Of course the answer led me, always, back to that Knights of Columbus pin that he wore. But that was not a real answer and therefore it did not satisfy me.

Then I began to do some research work in the field of religion. I began to study both Catholicism and Protestantism until I had traced both back to their beginning, a line of procedure which I must confess brought me more understanding of the problems of life than I had gathered from all other sources. For one thing it disclosed the fact that Catholicism and Protestantism differ more in form than they do in effect; that both are founded on exactly the same cause, which is Christianity.

But this was by no means all, nor was it the most important

of my discoveries, for my research led, of necessity, in many directions, and forced me into the field of biology where I learned much that I needed to know about life in general and the human being in particular. My research led, also, to the study of Darwin's hypothesis of evolution, as outlined in his Origin of Species, and this, in turn, led to a much wider analysis of the subject of psychology than that which I had previously made.

As I began to reach out in this direction and that, for knowledge, my mind began to unfold and broaden with such alarming rapidity that I practically found it necessary to—

Wipe the slate of what I believed to be my previously gathered knowledge, and to unlearn much that I had previously believed to be truth.

Comprehend the meaning of that which I have just stated!

Imagine yourself suddenly discovering that most of your philosophy of life had been built of bias and prejudice, making it necessary for you to acknowledge that, far from being a finished scholar, you were barely qualified to become an intelligent student!

That was exactly the position in which I found myself, with respect to many of what I believed to be sound fundamentals of life; but of all the discoveries to which this research led, none was more important than that of the relative importance of physical and social heredity, for it was this discovery that disclosed the cause for my action when I turned away from a man whom I did not know, on the occasion that I have described.

It was this discovery that disclosed to me how and where I acquired my views of religion, of politics, of economics and many other equally important subjects, and I both regret and rejoice to state that I found most of my views on these subjects without support by even a reasonable hypothesis, much less sound facts or reason.

I then recalled a conversation between the late Senator Robert L. Taylor and myself, in which we were discussing the subject of politics. It was a friendly discussion, as we were of the same political faith, but the Senator asked me a question for which I never forgave him until I began the research to which I have referred.

"I see that you are a very staunch Democrat," said he, "and I wonder if you know why you are?"

I thought of the question for a few seconds, then blurted out this reply:

"I am a Democrat because my father was one, of course!"

With a broad grin on his face the Senator then nailed me with this rejoinder:

"Just as I thought! Now wouldn't you be in a bad fix if your father had been a horse-thief?"

It was many years later, after I began the research work herein described, that I understood the real meaning of Senator Taylor's joke. Too often we hold opinions that are based upon no sounder foundation than that of what someone else believes.

That you may have a detailed illustration of the far-reaching effects of one of the important principles uncovered by the incident to which I have referred, and—

That you may learn how and where you acquired your philosophy of life, in general;

That you may trace your prejudices and your biases to their original source;

That you may discover, as I discovered, how largely you are the result of the training you received before you reached the age of fifteen years—

I will now quote the full text of a plan which I submitted to Mr. Edward Bok's Committee, The American Peace Award, for the abolition of war. This plan covers not only the most important of the principles to which I refer, but, as you will observe, it shows how the principle of organized effort may be applied to one of the most important of the world's problems, and at the same time gives you a more comprehensive idea of how to apply this principle in the attainment of your definite chief aim.

HOW TO ABOLISH WAR

Before offering this plan for the prevention of war, it seems necessary to sketch briefly a background that will clearly describe the principle which constitutes the warp and the woof of the plan.

The causes of war may be properly omitted for the reason that they have but little, if any, relation to the principle through which war may be prevented.

The beginning of this sketch deals with two important factors which constitute the chief controlling forces of civilization. One is physical heredity and the other is social heredity.

The size and form of the body, the texture of the skin, the color of the eyes, and the functioning power of the vital organs are all the result of physical heredity; they are static and fixed and cannot be changed, for they are the result of a million years of evolution; but by far the most important part of what we are is the result of social heredity, and came to us from the effects of our environment and early training.

Our conception of religion, politics, economics, philosophy and other subjects of a similar nature, including war, is entirely the result of those dominating forces of our environment and training.

The Catholic is a Catholic because of his early training, and the Protestant is a Protestant for the same reason; but this is hardly stating the truth with sufficient emphasis, for it might be properly said that the Catholic is a Catholic and the Protestant is a Protestant because he cannot help it! With but few exceptions the religion of the adult is the result of his religious training during the years between four and fourteen when his religion was forced upon him by his parents or those who had control of his schooling.

A prominent clergyman indicated how well he understood the principle of social heredity when he said: "Give me the control of the child until it is twelve years old and you can teach it any religion you may please after that time, for I will have planted my own religion so deeply in its mind that no power on earth could undo my work."

The outstanding and most prominent of man's beliefs are those which were forced upon him, or which he absorbed of his own volition, under highly emotionalized conditions, when his mind was receptive. Under such conditions the evangelist can plant the idea of religion more deeply and permanently during an hour's revival service than he could through years of training under ordinary conditions, when the mind was not in an emotionalized state.

The people of the United States have immortalized Washington and Lincoln because they were the leaders of the nation during times when the minds of the people were highly emotionalized, as the result of calamities which shook the very foundation of our country and vitally affected the interests of all the people. Through the principle of social heredity, operating through the schools (American history), and through other forms of impressive teaching, the immortality of Washington and Lincoln is planted in the minds of the young and in that way kept alive.

The three great organized forces through which social heredity operates are:

The schools, the churches and the public press.

Any ideal that has the active co-operation of these three forces may, during the brief period of one generation, be forced upon the minds of the young so effectively that they cannot resist it.

In 1914 the world awoke one morning to find itself aflame with warfare on a scale previously unheard of, and the outstanding feature of importance of that worldwide calamity was the highly organized German armies. For more than three years these armies gained ground so rapidly that world domination by Germany seemed certain. The German military machine operated with efficiency such as had never before been demonstrated in warfare. With "kultur" as her avowed ideal, modern Germany swept the opposing armies before her as though they were leaderless, despite the fact that the allied forces outnumbered her own on every front.

The capacity for sacrifice in the German soldiers, in support of the ideal of "kultur," was the outstanding surprise of the war; and that capacity was largely the result of the work of two men. Through the German educational system, which they controlled, the psychology which carried the world into war in 1914 was created in the definite form of "kultur." These men were Adalbert Falk, Prussian Minister of Education until 1879, and the German Emperor William II.

The agency through which these men produced this result was social heredity: the imposing of an ideal on the minds of the young, under highly emotionalized conditions.

"Kultur," as a national ideal, was fixed in the minds of the young of Germany, beginning first in the elementary schools and extending on up through the high schools and universities. The teachers and professors were forced to implant the ideal of "kultur" in the minds of the students, and out of this teaching, in a single generation, grew the capacity for sacrifice of the individual for the interest of the nation which surprised the modern world.

As Benjamin Kidd so well stated the case: "The aim of the state of Germany was everywhere to orientate public opinion through the heads of both its spiritual and temporal departments, through the bureaucracy, through the officers of the army, through the State direction of the press; and, last of all, through the State direction of the entire trade and industry of the nation, so as to bring the idealism of the whole people to a conception of and to a support of the national policy of modem Germany."

Germany controlled the press, the clergy and the schools; therefore, is it any wonder that she grew an army of soldiers, during one generation, which represented to a man her ideal of "kultur"? Is it any wonder that the German soldiers faced certain death with fearless impunity, when one stops to consider the fact that they had been taught, from early childhood, that this sacrifice was a rare privilege?

Turn, now, from this brief description of the modus operandi through which Germany prepared her people for war, to another strange phenomenon, Japan. No western nation, with the exception of Germany, has so clearly manifested its understanding of the far-reaching influence of social heredity, as has Japan. Within a single generation Japan has advanced from her standing as a fourth-rate nation to the ranks of nations that are the recognized powers of the civilized world. Study Japan and you will find that she forces upon the minds of her young, through exactly the same agencies employed by Germany, the ideal of subordination of individual rights for the sake of accumulation of power by the nation.

In all of her controversies with China, competent observers

have seen that back of the apparent causes of the controversies was Japan's stealthy attempt to control the minds of the young by controlling the schools. If Japan could control the minds of the young of China, she could dominate that gigantic nation within one generation.

NEED FOR APPLICATION OF SOCIAL HEREDITY IN TODAY'S WORLD

If you would study the effect of social heredity as it is being used for the development of a national ideal by still another nation of the West, observe what has been going on in Russia since the ascendency to power of the soviet government of Russia which is now patterning the minds of the young to conform with a national ideal, the nature of which it requires no master analyst to interpret. That ideal, when fully developed during the maturity of the present generation, will represent exactly that which the soviet government wishes it to represent.

Of all the flood of propaganda concerning the soviet government of Russia that has been poured into this country through the tens of thousands of columns of newspaper space devoted to it since the close of the war, the following brief dispatch is by far the most significant:

> RUSS REDS ORDER BOOKS. Contracts being let in Germany for 20,000,000 volumes. Educational propaganda is aimed chiefly at children. (By GEORGE WITTS)
>
> Special Cable to the Chicago Daily News Foreign Service. Berlin, German)', November 9th, 1920.
>
> Contracts for printing 20,000,000 books in the Russian language, chiefly for children, are being placed

in Germany on behalf of the soviet government by Grschebin, a well-known Petrograd publisher and a friend of Maxim Gorky. Grschebin first went to England, but was received with indifference when he broached the subject to the British government. The Germans, however, not only welcomed him eagerly but submitted prices so low that they could not possibly he underbidden in any other country. The Ullsteins, Berlin newspaper and book publishers, have agreed to print several million of the books at less than cost.

This shows what is going on over there.

Far from being shocked by this significant press dispatch, the majority of the newspapers of America did not publish it, and those that did give it space placed it in an obscure part of the paper, in small type. Its real significance will become more apparent some twenty-odd years from now, when the soviet government of Russia will have grown an army of soldiers who will support, to the man, whatever national ideal the soviet government sets up.

The possibility of war exists as a stern reality today solely because the principle of social heredity has not only been used as a sanctioning force in support of war, but it has actually been used as a chief agency through which the minds of men have been deliberately prepared for war. For evidence with which to support this statement, examine any national or world history and observe how tactfully and effectively war has been glorified and so described that it not only did not shock the mind of the student, but it actually established a plausible justification of war.

Go into the public squares of our cities and observe the monuments that have been erected to the leaders of war.

Observe the posture of these statues as they stand as living symbols to glorify men who did nothing more than lead armies on escapades of destruction. Notice how well these statues of warriors, mounted on charging steeds, serve as agencies through which to stimulate the minds of the young and prepare them for the acceptance of war, not only as a pardonable act, but as a distinctly desirable source of attainment of glory, fame and honor. At the time of this writing some well meaning ladies are having the image of Confederate Soldiers carved in the deathless granite on the face of Stone Mountain, in Georgia, in figures a hundred feet tall, thus seeking to perpetuate the memory of a lost "cause" that never was a "cause" and therefore the sooner forgotten, the better.

If these references to faraway Russia, Japan and Germany seem unimpressive and abstract, then let us study the principle of social heredity as it is now functioning on a highly developed scale here in the United States; for it may be expecting too much of the average of our race to suppose that they will be interested in that which is taking place outside of the spot of ground that is bounded on the north by Canada, on the east by the Atlantic, on the west by the Pacific and on the south by Mexico.

We, too, are setting up in the minds of our young a national ideal, and this ideal is being so effectively developed, through the principle of social heredity, that it has already become the dominating ideal of the nation.

This ideal is the desire for wealth!

The first question we ask about a new acquaintance is not, "Who are you?" but, "What have you?" And the next question we ask is, "How can we get that which you have?"

Our ideal is not measured in terms of warfare, but in terms of finance and industry and business. Our Patrick Henrys and our George Washingtons and our Abraham Lincolns of a few generations ago are now represented by the able leaders who manage our steel mills and our coal mines and our timber lands and our banking institutions and our railroads.

We may deny this indictment if we choose, but the facts do not support the denial.

The outstanding problem of the American people today is the spirit of unrest upon the part of the masses who find the struggle for existence becoming harder and harder because the most competent brains of the country are engaged in the highly competitive attempt to accumulate wealth and to control the wealth-producing machinery of the nation.

It is not necessary to dwell at length upon this description of our dominating ideal, or to offer evidence in support of its existence, for the reason that its existence is obvious and as well understood by the most ignorant as it is by those who make a pretense of thinking accurately.

So deeply seated has this mad desire for money become that we are perfectly willing for the other nations of the world to cut themselves to pieces in warfare so long as they do not interfere with our scramble for wealth; nor is this the saddest part of the indictment that we might render against ourselves, for we are not only willing for other nations to engage in warfare, but there is considerable reason to believe that those of us who profit by the sale of war supplies actually encourage this warfare among other nations.

THE PLAN

War grows out of the desire of the individual to gain advantage at the expense of his fellow men, and the smoldering embers of this desire are fanned into a flame through the grouping of these individuals who place the interests of the group above those of other groups.

War cannot be stopped suddenly!

It can be eliminated only by education, through the aid of the principle of subordination of the individual interests to the broader interests of the human race as a whole.

Man's tendencies and activities, as we have already stated, grow out of two great forces. One is physical heredity, and the other is social heredity. Through physical heredity, man inherits those early tendencies to destroy his fellow man out of self-protection. This Practice is a holdover from the age when the struggle for existence was so great that only the physically strong could survive.

Gradually men began to learn that the individual could survive under more favorable circumstances by allying himself with others, and out of that discovery grew our modern society, through which groups of people have formed states, and these groups, in turn, have formed nations. There is but little tendency toward warfare between the individuals of a particular group or nation, for they have learned, through the principle of social heredity, that they can best survive by subordinating the interest of the individual to that of the group.

Now, the problem is to extend this principle of grouping so that the nations of the world will subordinate their individual interests to those of the human race as a whole.

This can be brought about only through the principle of social heredity. By forcing upon the minds of the young of all races the fact that war is horrible and does not serve either the interest of the individual engaging in it or the group to which the individual belongs.

The question then arises, "How can this be done?" Before we answer this question, let us again define the term "social heredity" and find out what its possibilities are.

Social heredity is the principle through which the young of the race absorb from their environment, and particularly from their earlier training by parents, teachers and religious leaders, the beliefs and tendencies of the adults who dominate them.

Any plan to abolish war, to be successful, depends upon the successful co-ordination of effort between all the churches and schools of the world for the avowed purpose of so fertiliing the minds of the young with the idea of abolishing war that, the very word "war" will strike terror in their hearts. THERE IS NO OTHER WAY OF ABOLISHING WAR!

The next question that arises, "How can the churches and schools of the world be organized with this high ideal as an objective?" The answer is that not all of them can be induced to enter into such an alliance, at one time; but a sufficient number of the more influential ones can be induced, and this, in time, will lead or force the remainder into the alliance, as rapidly as public opinion begins to demand it.

Then comes the question, "Who has sufficient influence to call a conference of the most powerful religious and educational leaders?" The answer is:

The President and Congress of the United States.

Such an undertaking would command the support of the press on a scale heretofore unheard of, and through this source alone the propaganda would begin to reach and fertilize the minds of the people in every civilized country in the world, in preparation for the adoption of the plan in the churches and schools throughout the world.

The plan for the abolition of war might be likened to a great dramatic play, with these as the chief factors:

STAGE SETTING: At the Capitol of the United States.

STAR ACTORS: The President and members of Congress.

MINOR ACTORS: The leading clergymen of all denominations, and the leading educators, all on the stage by invitation and at the expense of the United States government.

PRESS ROOM: Representatives of the news-gathering agencies of the world.

STAGE EQUIPMENT: A radio broadcasting outfit that would distribute the entire proceedings half way round the earth.

TITLE OF THE PLAY: "Thou shalt not kill!"

OBJECT OF THE PLAY: The creation of a World Court, to be made up of representatives of all races, whose duty it would be to hear evidence and adjudicate the cases arising out of disagreement between nations.

Other factors would enter into this great world drama, but they would be of minor importance. The main issues and the most essential factors are here enumerated.

One other question remains, "Who will start the machinery of the United States government into action to call this conference?" and the answer is:

Public opinion, through the aid of an able organizer and leader, who will organize and direct the efforts of a Golden Rule Society, the object of which will be to move the President and Congress into action.

No League of Nations and no mere agreement between nations can abolish war as long as there is the slightest evidence of sanction of war in the hearts of the people. Universal peace between nations will grow out of a movement that will be begun and carried on, at first, by a comparatively small number of thinkers. Gradually this number will grow until it will be composed of the leading educators, clergymen and publicists of the world, and these, in turn, will so deeply and permanently establish peace as a world ideal that it will become a reality.

This desirable end may be attained in a single generation under the right sort of leadership; but, more likely, it will not be attained for many generations to come, for the reason that those who have the ability to assume this leadership are too busy in their pursuit of worldly wealth to make the necessary sacrifice for the good of generations yet unborn.

IDEAL USE OF GLOBALIZATON

War can be eliminated, not by appeal to reason, but by appeal to the emotional side of humanity. This appeal must be made by organizing and highly emotionalizing the people of the different nations of the world in support of a universal plan for peace, and this plan must be forced upon the minds of the oncoming generations with the same diligent care that we now force upon the minds of our young the ideal of our respective religions.

It is not stating the possibilities too strongly to say that the churches of the world could establish universal peace as an international ideal within one generation if they would but direct toward that end one-half of the effort which they now employ in opposing one another.

We would still be within the bounds of conservatism if we stated that the Christian churches, alone, have sufficient influence to establish universal peace as a worldwide ideal, within three generations, if the various sects would combine their forces for the purpose.

That which the leading churches of all religious, the leading schools and the public press of the world could accomplish in forcing the ideal of universal peace upon both the adult and the child mind of the world within a single generation, staggers the imagination.

If the organized religions of the world, as they now exist,

will not subordinate their individual interests and purposes to that of establishing universal peace, then the remedy lies in establishing a universal church of the world that will function through all races and whose creed will be based entirely upon the one purpose of implanting in the minds of the young the ideal of worldwide peace.

Such a church would gradually attract a following from the rank and file of all other churches.

And if the educational institutions of the world will not cooperate in fostering this high ideal of universal peace, then the remedy lies in the creation of an entirely new educational system that will implant in the minds of the young the ideal of universal peace.

And if the public press of the world will not cooperate in setting up the ideal of universal peace, then the remedy lies in the creation of an independent press that will utilize both the printed page and the forces of the air for the purpose of creating mass support of this high ideal.

In brief, if the present organized forces of the world will not lend their support to establishing universal peace, as an international ideal, then new organizations must be created which will do so.

The majority of the people of the world want peace, wherein lies the possibility of its attainment!

At first thought, it seems too much to expect that the organized churches of the world can be induced to pool their power and subordinate their individual interests to those of civilization as a whole.

But this seemingly insurmountable obstacle is, in reality, no obstacle at all, for the reason that whatever support this plan borrows from the churches it gives back to them, a thousand fold, through the increased Power the church attains.

Let us see just what advantages the church realizes by participation in this plan to establish universal peace as a world ideal. First of all, it will be clearly seen that no individual church loses any of its advantages by allying itself with other denominations in establishing this world ideal. The alliance in no way changes or interferes with the creed of any church. Every church entering the alliance will come out of it with all the power and advantages that it possessed before it went in, plus the additional advantage of greater influence which the church, as a whole, will enjoy by reason of having served as the leading factor in forcing upon civilization the greatest single benefit it has enjoyed in the history of the world.

If the church gained no other advantages from the alliance, this one would be sufficient to compensate it. But the important advantage that the church will have gained by this alliance is the discovery that it has sufficient power to force its ideals upon the world when it places its combined support back of the undertaking.

By this alliance the church will have grasped the far-reaching significance of the principle of organized effort through the aid of which it might easily have dominated the world and imposed its ideals upon civilization.

The church is by far the greatest potential power in the world today, but its power is merely potential and will remain so until it makes use of the principle of allied or organized effort; that is to say, until all denominations formulate a working agreement under which the combined strength of organized religion will be used as a means of forcing a higher ideal upon the minds of the young.

The reason that the church is the greatest potential power in the world is the fact that its power grows out of man's emotions. Emotion rules the world, and the church is the only organization which rests solely upon the power of emotion. The church is the only organized factor of society which has the power to harness and direct the emotional forces of civilization, for the reason that the emotions are controlled by FAITH and not by reason! And the church is the only great organized body in which faith of the world is centered.

The church stands today as so many disconnected units of power, and it is not overstating the possibilities to say that when these units shall have been connected, through allied effort, the combined power of that alliance will rule the world and there is no opposing power on earth that can defeat it!

POINTS TO REMEMBER
1. Intolerance is the chief cause of all wars.
2. Discover within yourself the root of your problems.
3. Move beyond worldly pursuits.

6

HABIT OF DOING MORE THAN PAID FOR

There are many objects, motives and people which arouse one's love-nature. There is some work which we do not like, some that we do like moderately, and, under certain conditions, there may be work that we actually LOVE!

Great artists, for example, generally love their work. The day laborer, on the other hand, usually not only dislikes his work, but may actually hate it.

Work which one does merely for the sake of earning a living is seldom liked. More often it is disliked, or even hated.

When engaged in work which he loves, a man may labor for an unbelievably long period of hours without becoming fatigued. Work that a man dislikes or hates brings on fatigue very quickly.

A man's endurance, therefore, depends very largely on the extent to which he likes, dislikes or loves that which he is doing.

We are here laying the foundation, as you will of course observe, for the statement of one of the most important laws of this philosophy, viz.:

A man is most efficient and will more quickly and easily succeed when engaged in work that he loves, or work that he performs in behalf of some person whom he loves.

Whenever the element of love enters into any task that one performs, the quality of the work becomes immediately improved and the quantity increased, without a corresponding increase in the fatigue caused by the work.

Some years ago a group of socialists, or perhaps they called themselves "co-operators," organized a colony in Louisiana, purchased several hundred acres of farm land, and started to work out an ideal which they believed would give them greater happiness in life and fewer of the worries through a system that provided each person with work at the sort of labor he liked best.

Their idea was to pay no wages to anyone. Each person did the work he liked best, or that for which he might be best equipped, and the products of their combined labors became the property of all. They had their own dairy, their own brick-making plant, their own cattle, poultry, etc. They had their own schools and a printing plant through which they published a paper.

A Swedish gentleman from Minnesota joined the colony, and at his own request he was placed at work in the printing plant. Very soon he complained that he did not like the work, so he was changed and put to work on the farm, operating a tractor. Two days of this was all he could stand, so he again applied for a transfer, and was assigned to the dairy. He could not get along with the cows, so he was once more changed, to the laundry, where he lasted but one day. One by one he tried every job on the works, but liked none of them. It had begun to look as if he did not fit in with the co-operative idea of living, and he was about to withdraw when someone happened to think of one job he had not yet tried—in the brick plant, so he was given a wheelbarrow and put to work wheeling bricks from the kilns and stacking them in piles, in the brick yard. A week's time went by and no complaint was registered by him. When asked if he liked his job he replied, "This ban chust the job I like."

Imagine anyone preferring a job wheeling bricks! However, that job suited the Swede's nature, he worked alone, at a task which called for no thought, and placed upon him no responsibility, which was just what he wanted.

He remained at the job until all the bricks had been wheeled out and stacked, then withdrew from the colony because there was no more brick work to be done. "The nice quiet job ban finished, so I yank I ban go back to Minney-so-tie," and back to "Minney- sotie" he went!

When a man is engaged in work that he loves it is no hardship for him to do more work and better work than that for which he is paid, and for this very reason every man owes it to himself to do his best to find the sort of work he likes best.

I have a perfect right to offer this advice to the students of this philosophy for the reason that I have followed it, myself, without reason to regret having done so.

This seems to be an appropriate place to inject a little personal history concerning both the author and the Law of Success philosophy, the purpose of which is to show that labor performed in a spirit of love for the sake of the labor, itself, never has been and never will be lost.

This entire lesson is devoted to the offering of evidence that it really pays to render more service and better service than one is paid to render. What an empty and useless effort this would be if the author had not, himself, practiced this rule long enough to be able to say just how it works out.

For over a quarter of a century I have been engaged in the labor of love out of which this philosophy has been developed, and I am perfectly sincere when I repeat that which I have stated elsewhere in this course, that I have been amply paid for my labors, by the pleasure I have had as I went along, even if I received nothing more.

My labors on this philosophy made it necessary, many years ago, for me to choose between immediate monetary returns, which I might have enjoyed by directing my efforts along purely commercial lines, and remuneration that comes in later years, and which is represented by both the usual financial standards and other forms of pay which can be measured only in terms of accumulated knowledge that enables one to enjoy the world about him more keenly.

The man who engages in work that he loves best does not always have the support, in his choice, of his closest friends and relatives.

Combating negative suggestions from friends and relatives has required an alarming proportion of my energies, during the years that I have been engaged in research work for the purpose of gathering, organizing, classifying and testing the material which has gone into this course.

These personal references are made solely for the purpose of showing the students of this philosophy that seldom, if ever, can one hope to engage in the work one loves best without meeting with obstacles of some nature. Generally, the chief obstacles in the way of one engaging in the sort of work one loves best is that it may not be the work which brings the greatest remuneration at the start.

To offset this disadvantage, however, the one who engages in the sort of work he loves is generally rewarded with two very decided benefits, namely; first, he usually finds in such work the greatest of all rewards, HAPPINESS, which is priceless, and secondly, his actual reward in money, when averaged over a lifetime of effort, is generally much greater, for the reason that labor which is performed in a spirit of love is usually greater in quantity and finer in quality than that which is performed solely for money.

DON'T DO MORE WORK, BUT BETTER WORK

There are more than a score of sound reasons why you should develop the habit of performing more service and *better service* than that for which you are paid, despite the fact that a large majority of the people are not rendering such service.

There are two reasons, however, for rendering such service, which transcend, in importance, all the others; namely,

First: By establishing a reputation as being a person who always renders more service and better service than that for which you are paid, you will benefit by comparison with those around you who do not render such service, and the contrast will be so noticeable that *there will be keen competition for your services, no matter what your life-work may be.*

It would be an insult to your intelligence to offer proof of the soundness of this statement, because it is obviously sound. Whether you are preaching sermons, practicing law, writing books, teaching school, or digging ditches, you will become more valuable and you will be able to command greater pay the minute you gain recognition as a person who does more than that for which he is paid.

Second: By far the most important reason why you should render more service than that for which you are paid; a reason that is basic and fundamental in nature; may be described in this way: Suppose that you wished to develop a strong right arm, and suppose that you tried to do so by tying the arm to your side with a rope, thus taking it out of use and giving it a long rest. Would disuse bring strength, or would it bring atrophy and weakness, resulting, finally, in your being compelled to have the arm removed?

You know that if you wished a strong right arm you could develop such an arm *only by giving it the hardest sort of use.* Take a look at the arm of a blacksmith if you wish to know how an arm may be made strong. Out of resistance comes strength. The strongest oak tree of the forest is not the one that is protected from the storm and hidden from the sun, but it is the one that stands in the open, where it is compelled to struggle for its existence against the winds and rains and the scorching sun.

It is through the operation of one of Nature's unvarying laws that struggle and resistance develop strength, and the purpose of this lesson is to show you how to harness this law and so use it that it will aid you in your struggle for success. By performing more service and better service than that for which you are paid, you not only exercise your service-rendering qualities, and thereby develop skill and ability of an extraordinary sort, but you build reputation that is valuable. If you form the habit of rendering such service you will become so adept in your work that you can *command* greater remuneration than those who do not perform such service. You will eventually develop sufficient strength to enable you to remove yourself from any undesirable station in life, and no one can or will desire to stop you.

If you are an employee you can make yourself so valuable, through this habit of performing more service than that for which you are paid, that you can practically set your own wages and no sensible employer will try to stop you. If your employer should be so unfortunate as to try to withhold from you the compensation to which you are entitled, this will not long remain as a handicap because other employers will discover this unusual quality and offer you employment.

The very fact that most people are rendering as little service as they can possibly get by with serves as an advantage to all who are rendering more service than that for which they are paid, because it enables all who do this to profit by comparison. You can "get by" if you render as little service as possible, but that is all you will get; and when work is slack and retrenchment sets in, you will be one of the first to be dismissed.

For more than twenty-five years I have carefully studied men with the object of ascertaining why some achieve noteworthy success while others with just as much ability do not get ahead; and it seems significant that every person whom I have observed applying this principle of rendering more service than that for which he was paid, was holding a better position and receiving more pay than those who merely performed sufficient service to "get by" with.

Personally I never received a promotion in my life that I could not trace directly to recognition that I had gained try rendering more service and better service than that for which I was paid.

I am stressing the importance of making this principle a habit as a means of enabling an employee to promote himself to a higher position, with greater pay, for the reason that this course will be studied by thousands of young men and young women who work for others. However, the principle applies to the employer or to the professional man or woman just the same as to the employee.

Observance of this principle brings a two-fold reward. First, it brings the reward of greater material gain than that enjoyed by those who do not observe it; and, second, it brings that reward of happiness and satisfaction which come only to those who render such service. If you receive no pay except that which comes in your pay envelope, you are underpaid, no matter how much money that envelope contains.

◆

My wife has just returned from the Public Library with a book for me to read. The book is entitled *Observation; Every Man His Own University*, by Russell H. Conwell.

By chance I opened this book at the beginning of the chapter entitled Every Man's University, and, as I read it through, my first impulse was to recommend that you go to the Public Library and read the entire book; but, upon second thought, I will not do this; instead, I will recommend that you purchase the book and read it, not once but a hundred times, because it covers the subject of this lesson as though it had been written for that purpose; covers it in a far more impressive manner than I could do it.

The following quotation from the chapter entitled Every Man's University will give you an idea of the golden nugget of truth to be found throughout the book:

> The intellect can be made to look far beyond the range of what men and women ordinarily see, but not all the colleges in the world can alone confer this power—this is the reward of *self-culture;* each must acquire it for himself; and perhaps this is why the power of observing deeply and widely is so much oftener found in those men and those women who have never crossed the threshold of any college but the *University of Hard Knocks.*

Read that book as a part of this lesson, because it will prepare you to profit by the philosophy and psychology upon which the lesson is built.

THE LAW OF INCREASING RETURNS!

Let us begin our analysis by showing how Nature employs this law in behalf of the tillers of the soil. The farmer carefully prepares the ground, then sows his wheat and waits while the Law of Increasing Returns brings back the seed he has sown, *plus a many-fold increase.*

But for this Law of Increasing Returns, man would perish, because he could not make the soil produce sufficient food for his existence. There would be no advantage to be gained by sowing a field of wheat if the harvest yield did not return more than was sown.

With this vital "tip" from Nature, which we may gather from the wheat fields, let us proceed to appropriate this Law of Increasing Returns and learn how to apply it to the service we render, to the end that *it may yield returns in excess of and out of proportion to the effort put forth.*

First of all, let us emphasize the fact that there is no trickery or chicanery connected with this Law, although quite a few seem not to have learned this great truth, judging by the number who spend all of their efforts either trying to get something for nothing, or something for less than its true value.

It is to no such end that we recommend the use of the Law of Increasing Returns, for no such end is possible, within the broad meaning of the word success.

Another remarkable and noteworthy feature of the Law of Increasing Returns is the fact that it may be used by those who purchase service with as great returns as it can be by those who render service, for Proof of which we have but to study the effects of Henry Ford's famous Five-Dollar-a-day minimum wage scale which he inaugurated some years ago.

Those who are familiar with the facts say that Mr. Ford was

not playing the part of a philanthropist when he inaugurated this minimum wage scale; but, to the contrary, he was merely taking advantage of a sound business principle which has probably yielded him greater returns, in both dollars and goodwill, than any other single policy ever inaugurated at the Ford plant.

By paying more wages than the average, he received more service and better service than the average!

At a single stroke, through the inauguration of that minimum wage policy, Ford attracted the best labor on the market and placed a premium upon the privilege of working in his plant.

I have no authentic figures at hand bearing on the subject, but I have sound reason to conjecture that for every five dollars Ford spent, under this policy, he received at least seven dollars and fifty cents' worth of service. I have, also, sound reason to believe that this policy enabled Ford to reduce the cost of supervision, because employment in his plant became so desirable that no worker would care to run the risk of losing his position by "soldiering" on the job or rendering poor service.

Where other employers were forced to depend upon costly supervision in order to get the service to which they were entitled, and for which they were paying, Ford got the same or better service by the less expensive method of placing a premium upon employment in his plant.

Marshall Field was probably the leading merchant of his time, and the great Field store, in Chicago, stands today as a monument to his ability to apply the Law of Increasing Returns.

A customer purchased an expensive lace waist at the Field store, but did not wear it. Two years later she gave it to her niece as a wedding present. The niece quietly returned the waist to the Field store and exchanged it for other merchandise, despite the fact that it had been out for more than two years and was then out of style.

Not only did the Field store take back the waist, but, what is of more importance it did so *without argument!*

Of course there was no obligation, moral or legal, on the part of the store to accept the return of the waist at that late date, which makes the transaction all the more significant.

The waist was originally priced at fifty dollars, and of course it had to be thrown on the bargain counter and sold for whatever it would bring, but the keen student of human nature will understand that the Field store not only did not lose anything on the waist, but it actually profited by the transaction to an extent that cannot be measured in mere dollars.

The woman who returned the waist knew that she was not entitled to a rebate; therefore, when the store gave her that to which she was not entitled the transaction won her as a permanent customer. But the effect of the transaction did not end here; it only began; for this woman spread the news of the "fair treatment" she had received at the Field store, far and near. It was the talk of the women of her set for many days, and the Field store received more advertising from the transaction than it could have purchased in any other way with ten times the value of the waist.

The success of the Field store was built largely upon Marshall Field's understanding of the Law of Increasing Returns, which prompted him to adopt, as a part of his business policy, the slogan, "The customer is always right."

When you do only that for which you are paid, there is nothing out of the ordinary to *attract favorable comment* about the transaction; but, when you willingly do more than that for which you are paid, your action attracts the favorable attention of all who are affected by the transaction, and goes another step toward establishing a reputation that will eventually set the Law of Increasing Returns to work in your behalf, for this reputation will create a demand for your services, far and wide.

Carol Downes went to work for W. C. Durant, the automobile manufacturer, in a minor position. He is now Mr. Durant's right-hand man, and the president of one of his automobile distributing companies. He promoted himself into this profitable position solely through the aid of the Law of Increasing Returns, which he put into operation by rendering more service and better service than that for which he was paid.

In a recent visit with Mr. Downes I asked him to tell me how he managed to gain promotion so rapidly, in a few brief sentences he told the whole story.

"When I first went to work with Mr. Durant," said he, "I noticed that he always remained at the office long after all the others had gone home for the day, and I made it my business to stay there, also. No one asked me to stay, but I thought someone should be there to give Mr. Durant any assistance he might need. Often he would look around for someone to bring him a letter file, or render some other trivial service, and *always he found me there ready to serve him*. He got into the habit of calling on me; that is about all there is to the story."

"He got into the habit of calling on me!"

Read that sentence again, for it is full of meaning of the richest sort.

Why did Mr. Durant get into the habit of calling on Mr. Downes? Because *Mr. Downes made it his business to be on hand where he would be seen.* He deliberately placed himself in Mr. Durant's way in order that he might render service that would place the Law of Increasing Returns back of him.

Was he told to do this? *No!*

Was he paid to do it? *Yes!* He was paid by the opportunity

it offered for him to bring himself to the attention of the man who had it within his power to promote him.

We are now approaching the most important part of this lesson, because this is an appropriate place at which to suggest that *you* have the same opportunity to make use of the Law of Increasing Returns that Mr. Downes had, and you can go about the application of the Law in exactly the same way that he did, *by being on hand and ready to volunteer your services in the performance of work which others may shirk because they are not paid to do it.*

Stop! Don't say it—don't even think it if you have the slightest intention of springing that old timeworn phrase entitled, "But my *employer is different.*"

Of course he is different. All men are different in most respects, but they are very much alike in this—they are somewhat *selfish;* in fact they are selfish enough not to want a man such as Carol Downes to cast his lot with their competitor, and this very selfishness may be made to serve you as an asset and not as a liability *if—*

You have the good judgment to make yourself so useful that the person to whom you sell your services cannot get along without you.

One of the most advantageous promotions I ever received came about through an incident which seemed so insignificant that it appeared to be unimportant. One Saturday afternoon, a lawyer, whose office was on the same floor as that of my employer, came in and asked if I knew where he could get a stenographer to do some work which he was compelled to finish that day.

I told him that all of our stenographers had gone to the ball game, and that I would have been gone had he called five minutes later, but that I would be very glad to stay and do his work as I could go to a ball game any day and his work had to be done then.

I did the work for him, and when he asked how much he owed me I replied, "Oh, about a thousand dollars, as long as it is you; if it were for anyone else, I wouldn't charge anything." He smiled, and thanked me.

Little did I think, when I made that remark, that he would ever pay me a thousand dollars for that afternoon's work, but *he did!* Six months later, after I had entirely forgotten the incident, he called on me again, and asked how much salary I was receiving. When I told him he informed me that he was ready to pay me that thousand dollars which I had laughingly said I would charge him for the work I had performed for him and he *did pay it* by giving me a position at a thousand dollars a year increase in salary.

Unconsciously, I had put the Law of Increasing Returns to work in my behalf that afternoon, by giving up the ball game and rendering a service which was obviously rendered out of a desire to be helpful and not for the sake of a monetary consideration.

It was not my duty to give up my Saturday afternoon, but—

It was my *privilege!*

Furthermore, it was a profitable privilege, because it yielded me a thousand dollars in cash and a much more responsible position than the one I had formerly occupied.

It was Carol Downes' *duty* to be on hand until the usual quitting time, but it was his *privilege* to remain at his post after the other workers had gone, and that privilege properly exercised brought him greater responsibilities and a salary that yields him more in a year than he would have made in a lifetime in the position he occupied before he exercised the privilege.

I have been thinking for more than twenty-five years of this *privilege* of performing more service and better service than that for which we are paid, and my thoughts have led me to the conclusion that a single hour devoted each day to rendering service for which we are not paid, can be made to yield bigger returns than we received from the entire remainder of the day the day during which we are merely performing our *duty.*

◆

By the very nature of the subject of this lesson it can never be finished, for it leads into the heart of all human activities. Its purpose is to cause you to take the fundamentals upon which it is based and use them as a stimulus that will cause your mind to unfold, thereby releasing the latent forces that are yours.

This lesson was not written for the purpose of teaching you, but it was intended as a means of causing you to teach yourself one of the great truths of life. It was intended as a source of education, in the true sense of educing, drawing out, developing from within, those forces of mind which are available for your use.

When you deliver the best service of which you are capable, striving each time to excel all your previous efforts, you are making use of the highest form of education. Therefore, when you render more service and better service than that for which you are paid, you, more than anyone else, are profiting by the effort.

It is only through the delivery of such service that mastery in your chosen field of endeavor can be attained. For this reason you should make it a part of your *definite chief aim* to endeavor to surpass all previous records in all that you do. Let this become a part of your daily habits, and follow it with the same regularity with which you eat your meals.

Make it your business to render more service and better service than that for which you are paid, and lo! before you realize what has happened, you will find that THE WORLD IS WILLINGLY PAYING YOU FOR MORE THAN YOU DO!

Compound interest upon compound interest is the rate that you will be paid for such service. Just how this pyramiding of gains takes place is left entirely to you to determine.

Now, what are you going to do with that which you have learned from this lesson? and when? and how? and why? This lesson can be of no value to you unless it moves you to adopt and use the knowledge it has brought you.

Knowledge becomes POWER only through organization and USE! Do not forget this.

You can never become a Leader without doing more than you are paid for, and you cannot become successful without developing leadership in your chosen occupation.

POINTS TO REMEMBER

1. Every man owes it to himself to do his best to find the sort of work he likes best.
2. By performing more services than that you are paid, you can set your own goals.
3. Apply the Law of Increasing Returns.

7

MAINTAIN SOUND HEALTH

You want to get the greatest vigor and fullest use from your body. You can do this if you understand two important points:

1. Your body and mind are one, effectively a mind-body.
2. Your mind-body is, in turn, at one with nature.

The health of your mind and body cannot be separated. Anything that affects the soundness of your mind will affect your body, and anything that affects your body will touch your mind. This is why I refer to you as a mind-body.

But you are also affected by your environment, subject to natural laws that govern your mind-body just as much as they affect trees, mountains, birds, and beasts.

Understanding the way in which you can maintain a sound mind-body depends, therefore, on understanding the way nature works. You must learn to work with natural forces, not fight them.

THE RHYTHMS OF LIFE

When you consider the waves of the ocean, the passing of the seasons, the waxing and waning of the moon, you will see that nature moves in rhythms. There is even a rhythm in your own life from birth through childhood and adolescence to full maturity, old age, and finally birth of a new generation. Light, energy, and matter are made up of waves, either moving out in their own rhythm or bound, like a neutron, around the fixed point of the nucleus of the atom.

Nothing about life is static. Movement is constant and rhythmic (though sometimes that rhythm is too large or small for us to perceive immediately). This is one reason why we enjoy music, for it reflects the rhythms and waves of our experience. You must learn to bend and sway with the rhythms of life, not to stand fixed and immobile against them. A sandy beach moves and changes with the rhythms of the waves and lasts for eons; a breakwater is soon destroyed.

Take a look at your life. Is it rhythmical? Are you following work with play, mental effort with physical effort, eating with fasting, seriousness with humor, sex with transmutation of sex into creative effort?

Your subconscious does its best work on your behalf while your conscious mind is at rest. True inspiration most often comes after your subconscious has been given a task and while your conscious mind is then occupied elsewhere—that is, while your mind is playing.

Archimedes had struggled with the complex problem of determining the relative mass of two objects without finding a solution. It was only when he decided to relax and slip into his bath that his subconscious was stimulated by the water he displaced in his tub. He sprang from his bath with that now-famous cry of "Eureka!" and the solution he had been seeking. Are you giving your mind a chance to relax by playing?

Interference with normal rhythmical patterns produces so many problems. If you don't give your mind a rhythm of work and relaxation, your body will be so constantly stimulated that you will likely end up with a stress-related disorder. And without highs and lows, the things that you value begin to pale. Your past failures are what makes success sweet.

You don't really want continuous happiness, for then your happiness would seem dull. One of the major goals of marriage counseling is getting couples to understand that there is no such thing as being constantly in love. People in love have a series of loves, like waves on the oceans. In the troughs they are neutral in their feelings, but troughs make the peaks of the waves so much more poignant. As in life, not all the ocean's waves are of the same intensity; there are a few for each of us that reach great heights, and it is the memory and exhilaration of these moments that we store up to call upon when the going gets difficult.

You have to learn to understand the waves and rhythms in your life and to live within those rhythms in order to be in harmony with the world.

THE INFLUENCE OF YOUR MIND

Just as you have to understand nature as a complex whole, moving with its own rhythms, you have to understand that your mind and body are a whole, each influencing the other.

Humans are the only thinking creatures, and this power allows you to modify your world and to learn its laws. You need only to conceive the idea and believe in it to achieve the idea.

This is the story of all the successful people who have changed the path of civilization. It took countless hundreds of millions of years for evolution to develop from all the animals that walked or swam a bird that could fly. Yet the Wright brothers, with childlike faith in their own idea, had human beings airborne in a mere twenty years. That is the power of the mind, demonstrated to us by experience and reinforced by the words of countless prophets in touch with Infinite Intelligence. Christ himself said, "All things are possible even unto the end of the world."

Your mind has the higher function in your mind-body. Your body is an exquisitely functioning machine for carrying your mind about and executing the dictates of this powerhouse. A smoothly functioning mind is necessary to a smoothly functioning body.

Some people have bodies that are limited. They can move, see, or speak only with difficulty or not at all. Yet the power of their minds allows them to live full creative lives. Helen Keller is a marvelous example, as are Beethoven and Edison, both of whom suffered from severely impaired hearing. Franklin Roosevelt was barely able to stand on his own, yet he inspired and led our country through the greatest depression and war we ever faced. Senator Bob Dole's arm was permanently injured in World War II, but that has not stopped him from becoming one of our most influential political leaders.

The story of civilization is punctuated with great'ess achieved by individuals in spite of physical limitations because these people possessed smoothly functioning minds. On the wings of a definite major purpose, faith, enthusiasm, and a positive mental attitude, they rose farther and farther from any despair over their limitations toward great heights of brilliant achievement. That is the influence of the mind.

ESSENTIALS OF SUCCESS AND HAPPINESS

Many of the essential principles of success are also essential to a smoothly functioning mind. A definite major purpose and a plan for carrying it out keep you from vacillating in your efforts. Think of a situation in which you were part of a smoothly functioning plan. You were content with the way the situation was handled. You felt at ease and comfortable. Your mind is always satisfied with the harmony produced by a well-organized plan. Anxiety develops from a poorly organized plan.

Controlled attention, self-discipline, accurate thinking, personal initiative, learning from defeat, and going the extra mile all are mental tools you can use to organize and carry out your plan. They give you satisfaction both in the achievement of each step of your plan and in your overall progress. Satisfactions are important foods for a healthy mind.

Probably the most important single quality for sound mental health is a positive mental attitude and all that it entails. Two of the greatest destructive forces in the human mind are fear and its close partner, anxiety. They kill enthusiasm, destroy faith, blind vision, blunt creative effort, and dispel harmony and peace of mind—all qualities necessary for a positive mental attitude and sound mental health.

THE FORCE OF FEAR

Fear and anxiety produce unharmonious, irritated restlessness in your mind that leads to serious mental maladjustment and produces its counterpart in the body in the form of serious disease, perhaps even death. There is a growing awareness in the healing professions that many human ailments are either the product of mental distress or greatly exacerbated by it.

The list of diseases that are brought on by stress is long, varied, and growing: allergies, asthma, skin disease, hypertension, cardiac problems, arthritis, colitis, and immune disorders.

Some hayfever sufferers start sneezing and itching at the

sight of goldenrod in a vase. Tell them the plant is artificial, and their symptoms clear. This is a simple example of how the mind can affect the body negatively.

You must replace fear with understanding and faith in yourself. To do this, let's look at how fear affects the mechanisms of your body.

Temporary, fleeting fear is a normal and important function. It gets you to move out of the way of an oncoming train or keeps you from walking too near a cliff by momentarily focusing your attention—your mind—on a problem. Once the problem is over, this kind of fear is forgotten.

Fear also focuses your bodily functions on a threat. That old story of a cave dweller frightened by a sound in the night is a good illustration. Instantaneously the heart begins pumping faster; blood is diverted from the digestion for use by the muscles; the blood vessels serving the muscles dilate to handle increased volume, while those near the skin contract so that less blood is lost in case of a cut. Hearing becomes more acute; the pupils dilate to take in more light; the adrenaline gland unleashes a torrent of stimulant to provide strength for a fight.

All this is preparation for surviving a battle or chase. The ensuing battle uses up the adrenaline and exhausts the other bodily systems so that they step down from their heightened readiness. Blood leaves the muscles to return to digestive and other functions.

This is an extremely powerful response, one that kept our species alive over millions of years. But it is not intended to be a constant state, for it diverts the body from its normal functions. Still, some of us activate this response to some extent daily or even continually because we live in frequent fear.

You must work to eliminate the causes of those fears.

The fear of the loss of money: Have you set up a system to conserve and develop your assets?

The fear of ill health: Have you sought and followed worthwhile counsel?

The fear of loss of love: Have you put as much effort into increasing your beloved's affection as you would into cultivating an important business prospect?

The fear of death: Have you sought help and understanding to the point where fear is replaced by faith?

The list of fears is endless, yet to cultivate a positive mental attitude and develop a smoothly functioning mind that can live in harmony with itself and the world, you must conquer fear and anxiety.

If the same fears and anxieties recur in your mind constantly and are paralyzing your efforts, seek the help of a good professional counselor. You aren't admitting weakness by doing this; you are expressing maturity and commitment to your health and your definite major purpose. A brief period of therapy may mean years of happiness.

Remember that whatever your mind can conceive and believe, it can achieve. Isn't the person who is afraid of falling on the ice the one who falls? Repeating a fear over and over in your mind makes you more susceptible to the things you fear. You must vanquish fear before it vanquishes you.

THE FORCE OF A POSITIVE MENTAL ATTITUDE

The best way to remove fear from your mind is to replace it with PMA.

Émile Coué, the French psychologist, gave us a very simple but practical formula for building PMA and maintaining a health consciousness: "Every day, in every way, I am getting better and better." Repeat this sentence to yourself many times a day until your subconscious picks it up, accepts it, and begins to carry it out in the form of good health.

This is a simple yet astounding form of autosuggestion. It depends on your belief in the statement, but the best way to build that belief is to make the statement a part of your mental environment. Remember that your mind is strongly influenced by its environment, and by filling that environment with the right thoughts, you will come to believe them.

EATING HABITS

The purpose of food is to supply the body with the things it needs to maintain itself in good repair. Your eating habits must be guided by this goal alone.

Think of your digestive system as a factory. To function efficiently, it has to have a supply of a variety of materials in varying quantities. If you provide the wrong mix of materials, some jobs will never be completed, some will be done with jerry-rigged parts, and some materials will simply be stored up in every corner until the walls of the factory begin to swell. Finally the walls burst, the roof caves in, and the factory is either out of business or in need of serious and expensive repair.

Information about nutritional requirements continues to evolve as scientists work to understand more and more about the body. Pay attention to new information (but do not be swept along by fads) as it becomes available. In the main, however, some simple points will keep your diet balanced:

1. Fresh fruits and vegetables should make up the largest

portion of your meals. They supply complex mixes of vitamins and trace elements, and your body is designed to avail itself of them easily.

2. Complex carbohydrates, such as breads, grains, and potatoes, should be the next largest.
3. Protein, in the form of lean meats, fish, and dairy products, is important, but it should not be the center of your meals. Select small amounts of foods you enjoy, rather than gorge yourself on steak at every meal.
4. Avoid fats; limit your intake of butter and oils, and stay away from deep-fried foods. Also avoid sugars, like candy and colas, which provide little but calories.

Seek variety as well. Your body's nutritional needs run a wide gamut, and the best way to serve those needs without becoming a food chemist is to be sure that you eat a wide spectrum of foods. Don't say, "I can't eat that way," for all you are really saying is "I don't want to eat that way." It is a very glib bit of mental gymnastics to make yourself believe that it is impossible to do what is really only unappealing or different. Why should all your efforts for success stumble over your ill health because you don't like broccoli?

Never eat while angry, frightened, or worried. Your body is simply not in a position to make use of the food when it is on a defensive footing. Worse, you can make eating a habitual response to stress, which can lead to overweight.

Moderation in food and alcohol intake is important, both because your body can be overwhelmed by an excess of either and because overindulgence can become a trick to avoid dealing with some problem that urgently needs to be faced. If you find that you cannot control either, seek the help of professionals or a worthy organization like Alcoholics or Overeaters Anonymous.

RHYTHMS IN RELAXATION

Relaxation entails completely forgetting the worries and problems of the day. As desirable as this may seem, many people have trouble relaxing.

Your conscious mind selects objects on which to concentrate, and this concentration means the exclusion of other thoughts. You cannot just collapse into a chair and announce, "I am relaxing," because your mind will select some object of focus, most often the very item you wish to forget about for a time. You need to select an object of relaxation for your mind to concentrate on. It can be kite flying, gardening, reading a novel, or anything else which will absorb you.

Television and the corner bar are not the answers. Cultivate a variety of interests that take your mind to new places. Practicing controlled meditation will do wonders for your mental powers. Physical activity can be a terrific thing to immerse yourself in; not only do you relax your mind, but you strengthen your body.

Short periods of relaxation throughout the day can break tension and give your subconscious a chance to work. Read a magazine article; listen to a language tape; work on a crossword puzzle. This is not wasting time; it is keeping your mind in top condition through relaxation.

SLEEP

Your body needs time to rebuild and revitalize itself for the next day. It is sheer stupidity to try to increase your productivity by cutting your sleeping time. Six to eight hours a night are all you need. And remember that even while you sleep, your subconscious is working.

Insomnia is often caused by a failure to relax before going

to bed. Don't work until you drop. Instead wind down at the end of the day by doing something you enjoy that doesn't overstimulate you. (For this reason, exercise is not good just before you go to bed.) Perhaps quiet small talk with your spouse is all you need, or an easy routine of brushing your teeth, stretching for a few moments, or making your bed. A habit which signals your body that it is time for sleep is a valuable aid.

EXERCISE

Ideally your relaxation and play will include exercise. Relaxing and playing are important to your mind, while exercise, which is mostly beneficial to your body, can also be of great mental benefit.

You need to engage in aerobic exercise for a period of twenty minutes at least three times a week to keep your heart and lungs strong. The rate at which you exercise must be determined by your age and physical condition; trainers at any local gym or YMCA can explain this to you and help you design a simple exercise regimen that is neither expensive nor time-consuming. (How much time do you spend watching TV?) Consult your doctor before you begin any exercise program.

Exercise can be a tremendous mental and physical stimulant, clearing away sluggishness. It also teaches you persistence and concentration. Athletic training has become an important field for understanding human potential and has resulted in many techniques that can be applied to your quest for success.

Bill Bowerman was a first-class track coach at the University of Oregon for many years; when he conceived an idea for a better running shoe, the lessons he had learned in training himself and others were an important part of making Nike the number one American shoe manufacturer.

SEX AND SUBLIMATION

Sex is your most precious and constructive drive; it is also the most easily debased. Sex is behind all the creative forces that advance human destiny. Sex has built cathedrals, universities, and nations. Why? Because the desire for sex causes us to work to please others, and out of that work spring kindness and the understanding of others.

Sex is a completely natural desire. Do not fear or deny it. But realize that you must direct it, like all desires, to definite ends instead of letting it become an end in itself. If sex is all you want, you will do anything to get it, forgetting your faith in yourself, your definite purpose, and your moral standards.

When you want sex, remember that you cannot get something for nothing. The intimacy of sex is gained by constructive work at building a committed relationship. If you channel your desire for sex into creating and providing for that relationship, you will not only get what your heart desires but also attain the heights of achievement.

To work to your greatest good, sex and sublimation need to be alternated in a rhythmical pattern, just as work and play do.

EFFECTIVE MIND-BODY STIMULANTS

At any given time your mind-body may need a boost. Many of the best boosters are things you are already doing; you just need to be conscious of the effect they have and seek them out.

- Sexual expression or a sublimated sexual drive keys up the mind so that it works rapidly and well, with real inspiration.

- Love, the ultimate aim of sexual desire, serves a similar purpose; when the two are combined, they are unbeatable.
- Fanning your burning obsession is a strong stimulant.
- Work is a wonderful opportunity for creative expression. Do something small and definite, yet satisfying, like making a phone call or writing a thank-you note.
- A burst of exercise releases pent-up energy, drives away frustration, and stimulates the brain with increased blood and oxygen.
- A little play lets the subconscious go to work.
- Music is full of rhythms, beats, and pulses. You can select it to boost your enthusiasm or help you calm down.
- Friendship is a great stimulant. Talk your problems over with others. Laugh with them.
- Your children can inspire you. Build a strong relationship with them, and never neglect to spend as much time with them as possible. Teach your children a skill, and renew your self-confidence. Let your children talk to you, and renew your faith.
- Mastermind alliances are powerful stimulants. Seek out the enthusiasm and experience of other people when you need a boost. Mutual suffering causes people to pool their mind power and direct it to relieve that suffering.
- Autosuggestion implants the ideas you want in your mind. Use it whenever you need it.
- Faith and religion are stimulants of the noblest order. Turn to the assurances they offer you and renew your sense of purpose.

Your mental and physical health is inseparable. You cannot work to strengthen one without having a positive effect on the other. Your mind and your body are the navigator and the ship which carry you to the success you desire. Do everything you can to preserve, protect, and defend them.

> ### POINTS TO REMEMBER
> 1. Your mind and body are one.
> 2. Two of the greatest destructive forces in the human mind are fear and anxiety.
> 3. Your past failures are what makes success sweet.

8

LEARN FROM ADVERSITY AND DEFEAT

Throughout this book I've reminded you to look for the seed of an equivalent benefit in every defeat you experience. This isn't always easy when you've suffered a setback, but it is an important part of the science of personal achievement. The time to begin mastering this skill is now, instead of while you're licking your wounds.

Failure and pain are one language through which nature speaks to every living creature, pointing out mistakes. Animals may become timid so that they avoid a threatening situation when it arises again; you must become humble so that you can acquire wisdom and understanding. Realize that the turning point at which you begin to attain success is usually defined by some form of defeat or failure.

With this realization, you need not accept defeat as failure but only as a temporary event that may prove to be a blessing in disguise.

EVERYONE FACES DEFEAT

No one who has attained success has not met with some form of failure comparable with the scope of his or her success. Edison "failed" with more than ten thousand different attempts to create a lightbulb before he hit on the formula that worked. Jonas Salk tried countless different media to cultivate the polio virus for a vaccine before he discovered that monkey brain tissue did the job.

Debbie Fields founded the high-profile Mrs. Fields Cookies chain with a single store and expanded it worldwide very quickly. Too quickly, in fact. The costs of expansion crippled the company, and Fields found herself deeply in debt. She learned that trying to own and run all the stores was simply too much. Now she franchises operations instead of running them herself, and the company is profitable and growing once more.

Defeat should be accepted merely as a test which permits you to discover the nature of your thoughts and their relation to your definite major purpose. Knowing this modifies your reaction to adversity and keeps you striving toward your goal. Defeat is never the same as failure unless and until it has been accepted as such. Emerson said:

> Our strength grows out of our weakness. Not until we are pricked and stung and sorely shot at, awakens the indignation which arms itself with secret forces. A great man is always willing to be little. While he sits on the cushion of advantages he goes to sleep. When he is pushed, tormented, defeated, he has a chance to learn something; he has been put on his wits; on his manhood; he has gained facts; learned from his ignorance; been cured of the insanity of conceit; has got moderation and real skill.

Defeat, however, does not promise the full-blown flower of benefit, only the seed from which some benefit may be coaxed. You must recognize the seed, nurture, and cultivate it by definiteness of purpose; otherwise it will never sprout. Nature looks with disfavor on any attempt to obtain something for nothing,

You need to thank your faults when they are revealed to you because you cannot truly understand them until you have fought them.

ADVERSITY BECOMES A BLESSING

Milo C. Jones operated a small farm in Wisconsin. He was barely subsisting at it when disaster struck: He suffered a paralyzing stroke.

His relatives were so convinced that he was a hopeless invalid that they put him to bed and left him there. Unable to use his body, Jones turned to his mind. Almost immediately he had an idea that was destined to compensate him for his misfortune.

He summoned his relatives together and charged them with planting his entire acreage with corn. That corn would be used to feed a herd of pigs. Those pigs would be slaughtered and turned into sausage.

Within a few years Jones's sausage was being sold in stores all across the nation. You know it as Jones Farm sausage. Milo Jones and his family became wealthier than they had ever dreamed.

This happened because Jones was forced by adversity to turn to a resource he had never really used: his mind. He formed a definite major purpose and a plan for realizing it. He created a mastermind alliance with his family, and with applied faith they carried out the plan that a stroke had brought to a poor farmer.

When defeat overtakes you, don't spend your time counting your losses. Save it to count your gains and assets, and you will realize that they are greater than any loss you have suffered.

You may wonder why Milo C. Jones had to be overcome by a debilitating ailment before he discovered the power of his mind. Others might say that his compensation for that ailment was only financial and therefore not equivalent to his loss of mobility.

But Jones also received spiritual benefits in realizing the power of his mind and the strength of his family. His success, to be sure, did not restore control of his body. But it did give him control of his destiny, which is the highest form of personal achievement. He could have lived out his life in his bed, worrying about himself and his family. Instead he was able to bring them security they would otherwise never have known.

Prolonged illness, like any crippling defeat, often forces us to stop, look, and listen. We learn to understand that still, small voice which speaks to us from within and leads us to take inventory of the factors which have led to defeat and failure in the past.

Again Emerson points the way in these matters:

> A fever, a mutilation, a cruel disappointment, a loss of wealth, a loss of friends, seems [sic] at the moment unpaid loss, and unpayable. But the sure years reveal the deep remedial force that underlies all facts. The death of a dear friend, spouse, brother, lover, which seemed nothing but privation somewhat later assumes the aspect of a guide or genius; for it commonly operates revolutions in our way of life, terminates an epoch of infancy or of youth which was waiting to be closed, breaks up a wonted occupation, or a household, or style of living, allows the formation of new ones more friendly to the growth of character.
>
> It permits or constrains the formation of new acquaintances, and the reception of new influences that

prove of first importance to the next years; and the man or woman who would have remained a sunny garden flower, with no room for its roots and too much sunshine for its head, by the falling of the walls and the neglect of the gardener is made the banyan of the forest, yielding shade and fruit to wide neighborhoods of man.

Time is relentless in preserving the seed of an equivalent benefit that hides within a defeat. The best time to begin looking for that seed in a new defeat is now. But you can also examine past losses for the seeds they contain. Indeed, sometimes the weight of the loss prevents you from searching at the time. But now, with your increased wisdom and experience, you are ready to examine any loss for the lesson it can teach you.

THE MAJOR CAUSES OF PERSONAL FAILURE

To give you some perspective on the losses you face, I have below listed the most common and powerful causes of failure. When you recognize any that have hampered you, it is important that you do not berate yourself for their presence in your life. Instead you must resolve to do something about them, and do it now!

1. The habit of drifting through life without a definite major purpose
2. Meddlesome curiosity about other people's affairs
3. Inadequate education
4. Lack of self-discipline, manifested as both uncontrolled appetites and indifference to opportunity
5. Lack of ambition
6. Ill health that results from negative thinking and poor diet

7. Unfavorable childhood influences
8. Lack of persistence and follow-through
9. Negative mental attitude
10. Lack of emotional control
11. The desire to get something for nothing
12. Failure to reach decisions promptly and firmly when all the facts needed for the decision are available
13. One or more of the seven basic fears: poverty, criticism, ill health, loss of love, old age, loss of liberty, death
14. Poor selection of a spouse
15. Overcaution or the lack of caution
16. Poor choice of a vocation or occupation
17. Indiscriminate spending of time and money
18. Lack of control over the tongue
19. Intolerance
20. Failure to cooperate with others in a spirit of harmony
21. Disloyalty
22. Lack of vision and imagination
23. Egotism and vanity
24. Desire for revenge
25. Unwillingness to go the extra mile

That's quite a list. But the causes of failure are many, and often you will find more than just one has led to your down-

In my youth I founded a magazine in Chicago dedicated to exhorting readers to strive for success. I lacked the capital for this venture, so I entered into a partnership with my printer. The magazine was a success, and even though I had to work long, endless hours, I was happy.

But I was not paying attention. My success threatened another publisher, and without my knowledge he bought out my printer partner and took over my magazine. I was out of work and separated from my labor of love in a most humiliating way,

Many of the above causes for failure were responsible for my defeat. The most important was that I had neglected to cooperate with my partner in a spirit of harmony; I bickered with him often about trivial details of publication. When the opportunity came to be free of me—and to make a profit doing it—he jumped at the chance. My egotism and vanity were responsible for much of this, as were my general lack of caution in business affairs and my sharp tongue.

But—and this is an important "but"—I did manage to find the seed of equivalent benefit by seeing these flaws in my way of doing business. I left Chicago for New York, where I founded a new magazine, one over which I retained control. To achieve this end, I truly had to inspire cooperation in my new business partners, who were risking their money without the power my former partner had kept. I also had to be much more cautious in my business planning since I depended more deeply on my own resources.

The result was a magazine that, within a year, had more than twice the circulation of my previous venture. And it was as a part of my efforts to build the profits of that magazine that I conceived a series of correspondence courses which were the first codification of the science of personal achievement.

I stood at a fork in the road when I was dethroned from my Chicago magazine. I could have given up and returned to the quiet lawyer's job my wife's family urged on me. Instead I recognized the seeds of equivalent benefit in my defeat, and I nurtured that seed beyond my wildest dreams.

THE BENEFITS OF DEFEAT

- Defeat reveals and breaks bad habits, releasing your energies for a fresh start with better habits.
- Defeat supplants vanity and arrogance with humility, paving the way for more harmonious relationships.
- Defeat causes you to take inventory of your assets and liabilities, both physical and spiritual.
- Defeat strengthens your willpower by providing it with a challenge to greater effort.

Bodybuilders know that it isn't enough just to jerk the barbell up; it has to be returned to its original position twice as slowly as it was raised. This principle is known as resistance training; it requires more control and effort than the showy work of actually lifting the weight.

Defeat can be your resistance training. Every time you return to where you started, do it deliberately, concentrating on the process, so that you train yourself to make even stronger and more powerful progress the next time.

YOUR ATTITUDE TOWARD DEFEAT

Again and again I've stressed that your attitude toward defeat is crucial to mastering it. You can see it only as a loss or as a chance for gain.

The negative attitude toward defeat is effectively summarized by Shakespeare in Julius Caesar when the murderer Brutus says:

There is a tide in the affairs of men,
Which taken at the flood, leads on to fortune;
Omitted, all the voyage of their life
Is bound in shallows and in miseries.

> On such a full sea are we now afloat;
> And we must take the current when it serves,
> Or lose our ventures.

These are the words of a doomed man, a man who seals his doom by failing to recognize that there is never just one chance, never just one tide that leads on to fortune.

The positive attitude is very different. Consider this poem by Walter Malone, entitled "Opportunity":

> They do me wrong who say I come no more,
> When once I knock and fail to find you in;
> For every day I stand outside your door,
> And bid you wake and rise, to fight and win.
>
> Wail not for precious chances passed away;
> Weep not for golden ages on the wane;
> Each night I burn the records of the day;
> At sunrise every soul is born again.
>
> Laugh like a boy at splendors that have sped,
> To vanished joys be blind and deaf and dumb;
> My judgments seal the dead past with its dead,
> But never bind a moment yet to come.

Malone's vision of defeat is the one you will prefer when you have discovered that every defeat carries the seed of an equivalent benefit. Remember, "At sunrise every soul is born again." That rebirth is the opportunity to put defeat behind you.

Fear, self-limitation, and the acceptance of your defeat as final will cause you to be "bound in shallows and in miseries," as Shakespeare suggests. But these things can be overcome by applied faith, a positive mental attitude, and a definite major purpose.

If you accept defeat as an inspiration to try again with renewed confidence and determination, attaining success will be only a matter of time. The secret to this is your positive mental attitude.

Remember, a positive mental attitude attracts success. You need that attraction most when coping with defeat. Redouble your efforts to maintain and build your PMA when adversity strikes, and use your applied faith in yourself and your purpose to put your PMA into action. That is the fundamental lesson in learning from adversity and defeat.

POINTS TO REMEMBER

1. Do not accept defeat as failure but only as a temporary event that may prove to be a blessing in disguise.
2. Instead of focusing on your setbacks, maintain focus on your goal.
3. The major causes of failure and how to change your attitude towards it.

9

WISDOM ROBS DEATH OF ITS STING

THE MYSTERY OF DEATH

It may be difficult for most people to interpret Death as being anything but an unavoidable tragedy, but this limited view of the subject can be broadened by taking account of the overall plan of the universe, which is in a constant state of flux, constantly undergoing *eternal change*.

Man comes to the earth plane without his knowledge or consent, remains in the Great School of Life a little while, then passes into another plane of intelligence without his consent. It is not a part of the Creator's plan for man to live on the earth plane forever, and it would be tragedy if it were a part of the overall plan.

Could anyone think of anything more frightful than to be compelled to remain forever on this earth plane of struggle, where life itself depends upon eternal vigilance on the part of the individual?

The life span is something like the modern school system. We enter the kindergarten period, graduate from there into the grades, then into high school, and from there we enter the last stage by entering college. The major purpose behind man's brief interlude on earth seems to be that of education.

If there had been no device of Death, think of the evil men the world has known—men who would still be living and making life miserable for everyone—the would-be conquerors and self-appointed dictators who have sought, from the dawn of civilization, to enslave all mankind.

Death is but an extended form of sleep, during which the individual sheds his tired, worn out physical body for one that is inexhaustible and eternal. Therefore it is a circumstance over which the individual has no final control, and it should be accepted as such and dismissed from the mind.

Understand the Law of Change, which is a part of the universal system, and Death becomes understandable, and may readily be accepted as a necessity. There could not coexist in the universe an eternal Law of Change and eternal life on the earth plane.

The individual may fear death, dread to meet with it, and look upon it as a tragedy, but fortunately the individual is only a pawn in relation to the overall plan of the universe, and as such his desires and the means of their fulfillment are confined entirely to that brief interlude known as Life, over which the individual has been given a free hand, to spend his brief visit in whatever manner he pleases.

The attitude of the philosopher toward Death seems to be the sensible one. He accepts it as a circumstance over which he has but a slight, limited control; therefore, he adjusts himself to it in a neutral spirit of belief that when it comes he will be ready for it, and he then dismisses the subject and devotes his energies to making his life yield all the benefits he can *in connection with those circumstances over which he has control.*

The philosopher looks upon those who fear Death as offering insult to their Creator. And the philosopher accepts every circumstance which touches his life as grist for the Mill of Life, and promptly adjusts himself to all such circumstances in a manner best suited to enable him to bene t from them.

Some of the Great Miracles constitute the major impedimenta standing in the way of peace of mind of the majority of people. The purpose of this analysis of the Miracles of Life is to help the individual relate himself to them in a mental attitude which will change them from things to be dreaded, to circumstances which can be made beneficial to his interests.

Through this analysis of the Great Miracles, the "Worry Bird" (which most people feed unnecessarily) has been robbed of the food necessary to keep it alive, and the way has been cleared for peace of mind, based on the acceptance of all the circumstances of life, just as they are.

It is my hope that each of you who read this volume will be conditioned, upon finishing this chapter, to properly interpret and apply the principles set forth in subsequent chapters, which have been designed to help you relate yourself to the Miracles in a manner that will give you the greatest benefits.

When this hope shall have been realized, then you will have found peace of mind which will endure throughout the remainder of your life.

The statements I have made in this analysis are not important. *But the thinking on your part, which the statements may have inspired, is important!* For it may well be that the thinking thus inspired may give you a change of attitude toward Life which will make Life sweeter as the years grow fewer.

POINTS TO REMEMBER

1. The major purpose behind man's brief interlude on earth seems to be that of education.
2. Change your attitude towards death.
3. Understand the Law of Change and learn to coexist.

10

THE SIXTH SENSE

The thirteenth step to Riches, the final step, is known as the SIXTH SENSE, through which Infinite Intelligence *may* and *will* communicate voluntarily, without any effort from or demands by the individual.

This principle is the apex of *The Think and Grow Rich Philosophy*. The SIXTH SENSE is that portion of the subconscious mind which has been referred to as Creative Imagination. It has also been referred to as the "receiving set" through which ideas, plans, and thoughts flash into the mind. These flashes are sometimes called hunches or inspirations.

The Sixth Sense defies description! It cannot be described to a person who has not mastered the other principles of this philosophy because such a person has no knowledge and no experience with which the Sixth Sense may be compared. Understanding of the Sixth Sense comes only by meditation through mind development *from within*. The Sixth Sense most likely is the medium of contact between the finite human mind and Infinite Intelligence, and for this reason *it is a mixture of both the mental and the spiritual*. It is believed to be the point at which the human mind contacts the Universal Mind.

After you have mastered all of the success principles explained in this book, you will be prepared to accept as truth a statement which may otherwise be incredible to you, namely:

Through the aid of the Sixth Sense, you will be warned of impending dangers in time to avoid them and notified of opportunities in time to embrace them.

With the development of the Sixth Sense, there comes to your aid, to do your bidding, a "Guardian Angel," who will open to you at all times the door to the Temple of Wisdom.

Whether or not this is a statement of truth you will never know except by following the instructions described in the pages of this book or some similar method of procedure.

I am not a believer in nor an advocate of miracles, for the reason that I have enough knowledge of Nature to understand that *Nature never deviates from her established laws*. Some of her laws are so incomprehensible that they produce what appear to be miracles. The Sixth Sense comes as near to being a miracle as anything I have ever experienced, and it appears so only because I do not understand the method by which this principle is operated.

This much I do know—there is a power, or a First Cause, or an Intelligence, which permeates every atom of matter and embraces every unit of energy perceptible to the human mind, and this Infinite Intelligence converts acorns into oak trees, causes water to flow downhill in response to the law of gravity, follows night with day, and winter with summer, each maintaining its proper place and relationship to the other. This Intelligence may, through the principles of *The Think and Grow Rich Philosophy*, be induced to aid in transmuting DESIRES into concrete, or material, form. I have this knowledge because I have experimented with it—and have EXPERIENCED IT.

Step by step through the preceding chapters, you have been led to this, the last principle. If you have mastered each of the preceding principles, you are now prepared to accept *without being skeptical* the stupendous claims made here. If you have not mastered the other principles, you must do so before you may determine definitely whether or not the claims made in this chapter are fact or fiction.

While I was passing through the age of hero worship, I found myself trying to imitate those whom I most admired. Moreover, I discovered that the element of FAITH, with which I endeavored to imitate my idols, gave me great capacity to do so quite successfully.

I have never entirely divested myself of this habit of hero worship, although I have passed the age commonly given over to such. My experience has taught me that the next best thing to being truly great is to emulate the great, by feeling and action, as nearly as possible.

Long before I had ever written a line for publication or endeavored to deliver a speech in public, I followed the habit of reshaping my own character by trying to imitate the nine individuals whose lives and life's work had been most impressive to me. These nine were Ralph Waldo Emerson, Thomas Paine, Thomas A. Edison, Charles Darwin, Abraham Lincoln, Luther Burbank, Napoleon Bonaparte, Henry Ford, and Andrew Carnegie. Every night over a long period of years, I held an imaginary Council meeting with this group whom I called my Invisible Counselors.

The procedure was this. Just before going to sleep at night, I would shut my eyes and see in my imagination this group of men seated with me around my Council Table. Here I had not only an opportunity to sit among those whom I considered to be great, but I actually dominated the group by serving as the chairman.

Before eyebrows are raised, let me assure you that I had a very DEFINITE PURPOSE in indulging my imagination through these nightly meetings. My purpose was to rebuild my own character so it would represent a composite of the characters of my imaginary counselors. Realizing as I did early in life that I had to overcome the handicap of being born into an environment of ignorance and superstition, I deliberately assigned myself the task of voluntary rebirth through the method here described.

BUILDING CHARACTER THROUGH AUTOSUGGESTION

Being an earnest student of psychology, I knew, of course, that all individuals have become what they are because of their DOMINATING THOUGHTS AND DESIRES. I knew that every deeply seated desire has the effect of causing one to seek outward expression through which that desire may be transmuted into reality. I knew that self-suggestion is a powerful factor in building character, that it is, in fact, the sole principle through which character is built.

With this knowledge of the principles of mind operation, I was fairly well armed with the equipment needed to rebuild my character. In these imaginary Council meetings, I called on my Cabinet members for the knowledge I wished each to contribute, addressing myself to each member in audible words such as follows:

"Mr. Emerson, I desire to acquire from you the marvelous understanding of Nature which distinguished your life. I ask that you make an impression upon my subconscious mind of whatever qualities you possessed which enabled you to understand and adapt yourself to the laws of Nature. I ask that you assist me in reaching and drawing upon whatever sources of knowledge are available to this end.

"Mr. Burbank, I request that you pass on to me the knowledge which enabled you to so harmonize the laws of Nature that you caused the cactus to shed its thorns and become an edible food. Give me access to the knowledge which enabled you to make two blades of grass grow where but one grew before, and helped you to blend the coloring of the flowers with more splendor and harmony, for you alone have successfully 'gilded the lily.'

"Napoleon, I desire to acquire from you, by emulation, the marvelous ability you possessed to inspire men and to arouse them to greater and more determined spirit of action. Also to acquire the spirit of enduring FAITH, which enabled you to turn defeat into victory and to surmount staggering obstacles. Emperor of Fate, King of Chance, Man of Destiny, I salute you!

"Mr. Paine, I desire to acquire from you the freedom of thought and the courage and clarity with which to express convictions which so distinguished you!

"Mr. Darwin, I wish to acquire from you the marvelous patience and ability to study cause and effect, without bias or prejudice, so exemplified by you in the field of natural science.

"Mr. Lincoln, I desire to build into my own character the keen sense of justice, the untiring spirit of patience, the sense of humor, the human understanding, and the tolerance which were your distinguishing characteristics.

"Mr. Carnegie, I am already indebted to you for my choice of a life's work, which has brought me great happiness and peace of mind. I wish to acquire a thorough understanding of the principles of *organized effort* which you used so effectively in the building of a great industrial enterprise. "Mr. Ford, you have been among the most helpful of the people who have supplied much of the material essential to my work. I wish to acquire your spirit of persistence, the determination, poise, and self-confidence which have enabled you to master poverty and to organize, unify, and simplify human effort, so that I may help others to follow in your footsteps.

"Mr. Edison, I have seated you nearest to me, at my right, because of the personal cooperation you have given me during my research into the causes of success and failure. I wish to acquire from you the marvelous spirit of FAITH with which you have uncovered so many of Nature's secrets, the spirit of unremitting toil with which you have so often wrested victory from defeat."

My method of addressing the members of the imaginary Cabinet would vary according to the traits of character in which I was for the moment most interested in acquiring. I studied the records of their lives with painstaking care. After some months of this nightly procedure, I was astounded by the discovery that these imaginary figures became apparently real.

Each of these nine men developed individual characteristics, which surprised me. For example, Lincoln developed the habit of always being late, then walking around in solemn parade. When he came, he walked very slowly with his hands clasped behind him, and once in a while, he would stop as he passed and rest his hand momentarily upon my shoulder. He always wore an expression of seriousness upon his face. Rarely did I see him smile. The cares of a sundered nation made him grave.

That was not true of the others. Burbank and Paine often indulged in witty repartee which seemed at times to shock the other members of the Cabinet. One night Paine suggested that I prepare a lecture on "The Age of Reason" and deliver it from the pulpit of a church which I formerly attended. Many around the table laughed heartily at the suggestion. Not Napoleon! He drew his mouth down at the corners and groaned so loudly that all turned and looked at him with amazement. To him the church was but a pawn of the state, not to be reformed, but to be used as a convenient inciter to mass activity by the people.

On one occasion Burbank was late. When he came, he was excited with enthusiasm and explained that he had been late because of an experiment he was conducting, through which he hoped to be able to grow apples on any sort of tree. Paine chided him by reminding him that it was an apple which started all the trouble between man and woman. Darwin chuckled heartily as he suggested that Paine should watch out for little serpents when he went into the forest to gather apples, as they had the habit of growing into big snakes. Emerson observed, "No serpents, no apples," and Napoleon remarked, "No apples, no state!"

Lincoln developed the habit of always being the last one to leave the table after each meeting. On one occasion, he leaned across the end of the table, his arms folded, and remained in that position for many minutes. I made no attempt to disturb him. Finally, he lifted his head slowly, got up and walked to the door, then turned around, came back, and laid his hand on my shoulder and said, "My boy, you will need much courage if you remain steadfast in carrying out your purpose in life. But remember, when difficulties overtake you, the common people have common sense. Adversity will develop it."

One evening Edison arrived ahead of all the others. He walked over and seated himself at my left, where Emerson was accustomed to sit, and said, "You are destined to witness the discovery of the secret of life. When the time comes, you will observe that life consists of great swarms of energy, or entities, each as intelligent as human beings *think* themselves to be. These units of life group together like hives of bees and remain together until they disintegrate *through lack of harmony*. These units have differences of opinion, the same as human beings, and often fight among themselves. These meetings which you are conducting will be very helpful to you. They will bring to your rescue some of the same units of life which served the members of your Cabinet during their lives. These units are eternal. THEY NEVER DIE! Your own thoughts and DESIRES serve as the magnet which attracts units of life from the great ocean of life out there. Only the friendly units are attracted— the ones which harmonize with the nature of your DESIRES."

The other members of the Cabinet began to enter the room. Edison got up and slowly walked around to his own seat. Edison was still living when this happened. It impressed me so greatly that I went to see him and told him about the experience. He smiled broadly and said, "Your dream was more a reality than you may imagine it to have been." He added no further explanation to his statement.

These meetings became so realistic that I became fearful of their consequences and discontinued them for several months. The experiences were so uncanny I was afraid if I continued them I would lose sight of the fact that the meetings were purely *experiences of my imagination.*

Some six months after I had discontinued the practice, I was awakened one night, or thought I was, when I saw Lincoln standing at my bedside. He said, "The world will soon need your services. It is about to undergo a period of chaos which will cause men and women to lose faith, and become panic-stricken. Go ahead with your work and complete your philosophy. That is your mission in life. If you neglect it for any cause whatsoever, you will be reduced to a primal state and be compelled to retrace the cycles through which you have passed during thousands of years."

The following morning, I was unable to tell whether I had dreamed this or had actually been awake, and I have never since found out which it was, but I do know that the dream, if it were a dream, was so vivid in my mind the next day that I resumed my meetings the following night.

At our next meeting the members of my Cabinet all filed into the room together and stood at their accustomed places at the Council Table, while Lincoln raised a glass and said, "Gentlemen, let us drink a toast to a friend who has returned to the fold."

After that, I began to add new members to my Cabinet, until soon it grew to more than 50, among them Christ, St. Paul, Galileo, Copernicus, Aristotle, Plato, Socrates, Homer, Voltaire, Spinoza, Kant, Schopenhauer, Newton, Confucius, Elbert Hubbard, Woodrow Wilson, and William James.

This is the first time that I have ever had the courage to mention this in writing. Heretofore, I have remained quiet on the subject because I knew from my own attitude in connection with such matters that I would be misunderstood if I described my unusual experience. I have been emboldened now to reduce my experience to the printed page because I am now less concerned about what "they say" than I was in the years that have passed. One of the blessings of maturity is that it sometimes brings one greater courage to be truthful, regardless of what those who do not understand may think or say.

Lest I be misunderstood, I wish here to state most emphatically that I still regard my Cabinet meetings as being purely imaginary, but I feel entitled to suggest that while the members of my Cabinet may be purely fictional and the meetings existent only in my own imagination, they have led me into glorious paths of adventure, rekindled an appreciation of true greatness, encouraged creative endeavor, and emboldened the expression of honest thought.

Somewhere in the cell structure of the human brain is an area which receives vibrations of thought ordinarily called hunches. So far, science has not discovered where this site of the Sixth Sense is located, but this is not important. The fact remains that human beings do receive accurate knowledge through sources other than the five physical senses. Such knowledge generally is received when the mind is under the influence of extraordinary stimulation. Any emergency which arouses the emotions and causes the heart to beat more rapidly than normal may, and often does, bring the Sixth Sense into action. Anyone who has experienced a near accident while driving knows that on such occasions the Sixth Sense often comes to one's rescue and aids, by split seconds, in avoiding the accident.

These facts are mentioned preliminary to a statement of fact which I shall now make, namely, that during my meetings with the Invisible Counselors I found my mind most receptive to ideas, thoughts, and knowledge which reach me through the Sixth Sense. I can truthfully say that I owe entirely to my Invisible Counselors full credit for such ideas, facts, or knowledge as I received through inspiration.

On scores of occasions when I have faced emergencies, some of them so grave that my life was in jeopardy, I have been miraculously guided past these difficulties through the influence of my Invisible Counselors.

My original purpose in conducting Council meetings with imaginary beings was solely that of impressing my own subconscious mind, through the principle of autosuggestion, with certain characteristics which I desired to acquire. In more recent years, my experimentation has taken on an entirely different trend. I now go to my imaginary counselors with every difficult problem which confronts me. The results are often astonishing, although I do not depend entirely on this form of counsel.

You, of course, have recognized that this chapter covers a subject with which a majority of people are not familiar. The Sixth Sense is a subject that will be of great interest and benefit to the person whose aim is to accumulate vast wealth or accomplish a great achievement of any kind, but it need not claim the attention of those whose desires are more modest.

Henry Ford undoubtedly understood and made practical use of the Sixth Sense. His vast business and financial operations made it necessary for him to understand and use this principle. Thomas Edison understood and used the Sixth Sense in connection with the development of inventions, especially those involving basic patents where he had no human experience and no accumulated knowledge to guide him, as was the case while he was working on the phonograph and the motion picture machine.

Nearly all great leaders, such as Napoleon, Bismark, Joan of Arc, Christ, Buddha, Confucius, and Mohammed understood and made use of the Sixth Sense almost continuously. The major portion of their greatness consisted of their knowledge of this principle.

The Sixth Sense is not something that one can take off and put on at will. Ability to use this great power comes slowly, through application of the other principles outlined in this book. Seldom does any individual come into workable knowledge of the Sixth Sense before the age of 40. More often, the knowledge is not available until one is well past 50 because the spiritual forces with which the Sixth Sense is so closely related do not mature and become usable except through years of meditation, self-examination, and serious thought.

No matter who you are or what may have been your purpose in reading this book, you can profit by it without understanding the principle described in this chapter. This is especially true if your major purpose is that of accumulation of money or other material things.

This chapter on the Sixth Sense was included because the book is designed to present a complete philosophy by which individuals may unerringly guide themselves in attaining whatever they ask of life. The starting point of all achievement is DESIRE. The finishing point is that brand of KNOWLEDGE which leads to understanding—understanding of self, understanding of others, understanding of the laws of Nature, and understanding and recognition of HAPPINESS.

This sort of understanding comes in its fullness only through familiarity with and use of the principle of the Sixth Sense, hence that principle had to be included as a part of this philosophy for the benefit of those who demand more than money.

Having read this chapter, you must have observed that while reading it you were lifted to a high level of mental stimulation. Splendid! Come back to this chapter again a month from now, read it once more, and observe that your mind will soar to a still higher level of stimulation. Repeat this experience from time to time, giving no concern as to how much or how little you learn at the time, and eventually you will find yourself in possession of a power that will enable you to throw off discouragement, master fear, overcome procrastination, and draw freely upon your imagination. Then you will have felt the touch of that unknown something which has been the moving spirit of every truly great thinker, leader, artist, musician, writer, scientist, or statesman. Then you will be in position to transmute your DESIRES into their physical or financial counterpart as easily as you may lie down and quit at the first sign of opposition.

FAITH VS. FEAR

Previous chapters have described how to develop FAITH through autosuggestion, desire, and the subconscious mind. The final pages of this book will present detailed instructions for the mastery of FEAR.

POINTS TO REMEMBER

1. The Sixth Sense is a mixture of both the mental and the spiritual.
2. The element of faith in your journey towards success.
3. Self-suggestion is the sole principle through which character is built.

11

IT IS UPTO YOU TO LIVE THE LIFE THE CREATOR GAVE YOU

The Golden Rule can be applied all-out in a way that will transform our economy for the better. When people are helped to turn their ideas into the realities of business and production, everyone in the United States will have more wealth and happiness. Most of us believe in man-made gods and man-made devils. Fear has no place in a well-lived life. Put your faith, not in a Creator who bosses you but One who makes it possible for you, as a human being, to win success by your own efforts.

Wealth now can be yours. Peace of mind now can be yours at the same time, but remember, this greatest of all wealth is known only to the person who possesses it.

"Help me find peace of mind," the rich man said.

This was some years ago. A trip across the country was not then a matter of six hours in a jet plane, but he had come across the country to talk to me. "I have everything money can buy," he said, "and I have lived long enough to find out that money cannot buy peace of mind. Please help me find it."

A good part of this chapter consists of what we discussed, and which I shall give to you in a conversational manner. First we went into everything this book has covered—I shall omit that part—and then we branched out into what has been for many years my most cherished project.

It is a business project—and a peace-of-mind project. It could bring joy and prosperity to millions of men and women, especially to those who need help in finding their places in life. It would work hand in hand with our American economy. It would not be a "make work" project, since it would provide services whose need is proved. It would make profit—that indispensable factor whose virtues have at length been recognized even in the Soviet Union. It would be a business project that first of all would be a human project devoted to creating wealth through sharing wealth.

A JOB FOR A DEDICATED MAN

"Before I tell you about my project," I said to my visitor, "I want to make it clear that it will need a dedicated man to get it going. A man who has plenty of money, plenty of time, and plenty of executive know-how, for all these are needed to turn the idea into reality. He would have to be a man who would go to work with no thought of what he would get out of his efforts. I say he would have to have plenty of money because he might lose some of his money—and he would also have to be psychologically suited to accept this fact without losing the peace of mind the project would give him."

"Tell me more," said the man from California.

"Well then, what I have in mind is a nationwide organization to be called 'The Golden Rule Industries of America.'"

The visitor looked puzzled. "Where does the Golden Rule come in?"

"Suppose you had just about enough money to live on, or even less, but you had a sound business idea you wanted to develop. What would you like someone to do unto you?"

"I surely would like someone to come along and give me capital!"

"That's what I meant. The Golden Rule Industries of America would devote itself to finding people who have sound business ideas, capitalizing those ideas and helping those people get started in their businesses. Then it would follow up with business management advice, as might be necessary. It would take care of the two major factors which make businesses fail—lack of capital and unsound management. It would fill those needs for honest people who want to get ahead but cannot fill those needs for themselves."

My visitor looked thoughtful. "There must be thousands of such cases."

"I am sure there are. Let me tell you of a few I know to exist.

"There is a young woman who is clever at designing. She wants to design and manufacture women's garments for the retail trade. Golden Rule Industries could set her up in business, make sure she got started on the right foot, and watch her grow. Eventually she would give employment to hundreds of people. Bear in mind that she, and every other person whom Golden Rule Industries aids with capital and business advice, will be a person who applies the Golden Rule to others, employees in particular. Golden Rule means that too."

"I see."

"A mechanic has built a model of an automobile which can be manufactured and sold for one thousand dollars. It will travel fifty miles to the gallon, will carry three people—ideal for the small family—and is so simple of design that its upkeep will be very small. Golden Rule Industries could set up this man in a small shop and let him expand as his business justifies.

Undoubtedly the entire automobile industry would respond with better cars at lower prices.

"A bright high school boy builds excellent model airplanes. He wants to develop his skill into a national business and employ other high school boys, after school, as his staff. Golden Rule Industries could help this youth and his friends start a business and develop it."

"That would be a wonderful head start toward a productive life!" my visitor exclaimed.

"It certainly would. I have in mind, too, a certain poor farmer. I have sympathy with poor farmers. This man wants to introduce the growing of a certain fiber plant now being developed in Africa, which can be grown in our southern states. There is an undoubted future in this, and Golden Rule Industries could provide this man with the land, machines and employees he needs.

"A young author has written a very creditable novel based on life in the mountains of Tennessee. He has not been able to get it published, but Golden Rule Industries could take it over for him and capitalize its publication if need be.

"A young lady stenographer has invented a chair so designed that it moves back and forth with the movement of the body and adjusts itself to fit the curvature of the back. This is a great idea. It will lessen fatigue, improve work, and should have a tremendous market. It would be a real pay deal for Golden Rule Industries."

"Where do these ideas come from?" my visitor wanted to know.

"Many of them represent cases I have handled for my clients. In my endeavors to help people stand on their own feet, I became aware of the many who have good ideas and plenty of ability, and need only capital and good management advice in order to get started. Now let me tell you of a rather special area in which Golden Rule Industries could do a world of good.

"In every prison there are many well-educated men capable of conducting business and educational courses for the benefit of the other inmates. This could result in these men being ready, willing and able to lead honest, useful lives when they are freed. A group of businessmen tried out this plan in the Ohio State Penitentiary, and it worked like a charm. The International Correspondence Schools contributed more than thirty-five thousand dollars worth of textbooks. The plan could be expanded greatly—and it is society that would profit. I have personally appropriated this idea and it is creating miracles of rehabilitation in many prisons.

"A mechanic has made a model of a prefabricated dwelling made of aluminum sections. Any able man with a couple of helpers can set up the walls and roof in a day's time and start living in the house with his family while he finishes the interior. There are similar houses on the market, but this one also can be taken down as easily as it is put up, and moved to another location, without damage to its components."

"There's profit in that idea," said the man from California.

"Yes, and I have a number of other ideas just as profitable. Many of them need only some way to get started despite the opposition of established interests who see only that their business world be affected, without seeing the benefit to the economy at large. Now let us digress from the business ideas themselves and look at Golden Rule Industries' general policy.

"Golden Rule Industries should be developed with the idea that it will pay a profit in itself as it goes along. I would, therefore, incorporate the idea of profit-sharing. Each enterprise would pay back to the Industries 10 per cent of its net earnings. Half of this amount would go to the Industries for the use of the capital and the business management. The other 5 per cent would be used as a payment on the original investment. When the investment was fully repaid, each enterprise would pay the Industries 5 per cent of its net earnings thereafter in return for management services and other services which might be necessary.

"You can see that this policy would create a revolving fund which could be used over and over to help more and more enterprises get started. But no enterprise would be bound forever to the Industries. After it paid back its capitalization, it could leave the Industries. We wouldn't want a monopoly. But I am quite sure that even if an enterprise left the Industries, it would continue on the Golden Rule basis of sharing the wealth it creates with its own employees, for it would be apparent by then that this is the way to make a business and its people prosper."

My visitor had arrived in my office with a woebegone face. Now he was vibrant and looked ten years younger. "That's great!" he exclaimed. "And I can see that one business after another would want to come in and join hands in such an undertaking. Why, it's the best way I ever heard of to prevent strikes and other labor troubles."

"I believe it would create harmony and peace of mind where those qualities are badly needed," I said. "And it would create all-important self-respect in giving people an opportunity to help themselves instead of feeding at the public trough at the expense of others. The plan would have a sweeping effect on our entire economy.

"Moreover, The Golden Rule Industries of America should operate its own radio and TV station. There would be no commercials. All the broadcasting time would be devoted to teaching people, in their own homes, all the essentials of personal achievement. People would find out at last that success is an inward matter which each of us must build within himself, rather than waiting for someone to hand him what he needs. We will have a nation that does not look for 'isms' to take care of it—a nation of people who will work hard to create wealth, in the happy confidence that they will receive a good share."

"Great heavens, man!" my visitor broke in. "You are talking about the millennium."

"No," I said, "I am presenting a practical plan to save this nation from destruction by the greedy who have not yet learned the necessity—and the virtue—of sharing riches.

"Golden Rule Industries would go beyond the transformation of industry in improving this land of ours. It would run a school for training men and women for public office—everything from dog-catcher to President. I hope this school eventually would attain such status as to make sure the voters may select public servants on the basis of their ability—instead of on their astuteness in swinging votes with the application of suitable amounts of money."

"Amen, amen!" said my visitor.

"Along with this school of political economy there would be a citizens' committee of men and women who are capable of examining and grading all candidates for public office. The people would once again come into full possession of their government."

"Great! But don't you think there would be a great deal of opposition to your plan—both industry-wise and government-wise? After all, you shut out a lot of nice, juicy opportunities for exploitation."

"I'd expect opposition," I replied. "Opposition is a healthy circumstance. It makes one either prove the soundness of his plan or discover its weaknesses. I'd expect to make adjustments as I went along.

"There are other features I have in mind for Golden Rule Industries which might provoke even more opposition. The power of the Industries' centralized buying would be such as to cause howls from those who think only of profit. When we helped our members buy homes of their own—as I believe should be done—there'd be screams of socialism—from other interests.

"When we helped Industries' members, including their employees, with such services as may be given by physicians, dentists, attorneys, even beauticians—and made sure they received the finest service at the lowest possible fees—the screams would rise to a crescendo. In the end, however, it would be recognized that the plan represents democracy operating on the highest possible scale of efficiency. All men who wish to live and let live will welcome this plan that adds so much to living. Our strength would lie in the fact that such people vastly outnumber the people who want to dominate and exploit others."

My visitor thought a moment. "And this would begin with finding people who have sound business ideas, and getting them into action."

"That is right. It would bring worthy beliefs of the human mind onto the plane of worthy achievement. The more we have in the world of this process, the better world we build."

My visitor sat a while. At last he arose and laid some large bills on my desk.

"I want you to have this honorarium in return for the help you have given me. I am going to swing into action with a new and better philosophy of life than any I ever have known in the past. I do not know if I am the man with the money, the time, the philosophy and the business experience to initiate Golden Rule Industries. But I see now what life can be when men cooperate in the production of goods and services for each other. I see why I made money but never found peace of mind. I see what has been lacking in my life, and I feel better, Dr. Hill. Yes, sir, I feel better than I have felt in years. You have done more for me than a number of doctors have been able to do."

My visitor never returned. Golden Rule Industries still remains a dream yet, in part, it is a dream I see coming true. Our economy grows less and less the hunting ground of the industrial pirate. It is only here and there that I see the development of co-operation, but I do see that groundswell of sharing the wealth, and it is this philosophy, based on the Golden Rule, which will keep America great; not the practice of handing out government doles to people who have done nothing to deserve them.

ABSTAIN FROM MAN-MADE INFLUENCES

We are approaching the end of this book. You see by now that the power of firm, free belief comes with an untrammeled mind: the power to turn what the human mind believes into what the human mind achieves rarely can be found by a man who is hemmed in with fear and misdirection.

There are some exceptions. You can see men in business still making money while they harm others in making it, but this type is nowhere nearly as prevalent as it was fifty years ago.

You can see exceptions elsewhere, too. Unfortunately, the human mind is capable of believing in man-made images which it sets up as Great Truths. This belief can lead to so-called achievement on its own plane; for instance, the achievement of great societies known as religions which teach that you will fry in Hell if you do not believe certain things.

I write here for strong people—for people who realize that

the most cherished beliefs nevertheless can be wrong in that they hinder the development of the human spirit. They claim to develop that spirit—but they develop it as much as a man's view of the world would be developed if he walked in a narrow alley between two high walls all his life.

Regardless of your emotions right now, surely you have been impressed by the fact that the Creator provided you with control over your own power of thought and made it impossible for any person to rob you of this privilege—unless you let him.

In my decades of research into the roots of personal achievement, I came across a book called *Catalogue of the Gods*. This book gave a brief description of each of the THIRTY THOUSAND man-made gods which men have worshiped since the beginning of civilization. Yes, THIRTY THOUSAND.

These sacred objects ranged all the way from the common angle-worm to the sun which warms our earth. They included almost every conceivable object between these two extremes, such as fish, snakes, tigers, cows, birds, rivers, oceans, and the genital organs of man.

Who made these objects into gods? Man himself. Which ones were authentic gods? Ask any worshiper and he would tell you, and eventually you would have a list of thirty thousand authentic gods, one just as authentic as another.

If I undertook to describe the miseries of mankind which can be laid at the feet (if they had feet) of those thirty thousand gods, and the fears and miseries and failures they have inspired in the minds of men, I would need more than one lifetime in which to do the job properly.

Man made a great step forward in his own behalf when he began to see a Creator, not gods, and removed this Creator from any connection with earthly objects. The ancient Hebrews performed this service for man. (One of the Egyptian kings appears to have come to the same conclusion some centuries before they did, but his priests saw to it that he died young.)

Yet what have we done with this belief? My own case is the one I know best. Until my father married the woman who saved me, the family in which I grew up was dominated by fear. It contributed to the support of an organization dedicated to maintaining that fear; it is known as the Hard-shell Baptists.

A preacher could visit our community only once a month, but on those occasions I was forced to listen to four or five hours of preachment. We were thundered at with pictures of a Hell waiting to receive us with fire and brimstone, and at times I could smell the stuff burning.

One night when I was seven or eight I dreamed I was down there chained to an iron post. My body was almost covered with a great pile of fresh brimstone. Here came Satan, swishing his tail, and with an evil grin he set fire to the brimstone. I awoke screaming. One needs no formal knowledge of psychology to know this is not good for any child. But when I tried to stay away from the church that gave me dreadful nightmares, I was thrashed without mercy.

THE CREATOR I KNOW

One day I overheard my stepmother say to my father: "The only real devil that exists in this or any other world is the man whose business is that of making devils." I accepted this statement instantly and never have departed from it.

I have taken pains to put into this book the fact that my father's prayers seemed to have focused powers of healing beyond medicine, which saved my life when I had typhoid fever. That was his time of faith, not fear.

In denying that I have anything to fear, I also deny that

anyone has knowledge enough to tell me anything definite about the spirit that rules the universe.

A theologian might say—although these days they are becoming wary of saying it: "Somewhere up there is Heaven, where God dwells, and all His acceptable children go there when they leave their earthly bodies, and gather around Him." A scientist might say: "I have turned my telescope outward into space in all directions. I have looked into space for distances equivalent to millions of light-years, but nowhere do I see the slightest trace of anything resembling Heaven."

The Creator whom I know is not separated from me by light-years nor by any other distance. I see evidence of His existence in every blade of grass, every flower, every tree, every creature on this earth, in the order of the stars and the plants which float out there in space, in the electrons and protons of matter, and most especially in the marvelous working principles of the human mind and the body within which it operates.

If you would rather speak of a force or a presence for a limitless intelligence rather than a Creator, it is the same. It is there. Is it affected by our worship? I doubt it. Can we sometimes attune ourselves so that we receive help from universal vibrations? This, I believe, is almost certainly true.

THE FINAL TRUTH

I do not even attempt to guess the over-all purpose or plan behind the universe. So far as I can tell, there is no plan for man except to come into this world, live a little while, and go. While he lives he is given the opportunity to make himself and his fellow men better beings, perhaps a more advanced form of man, as Lecomte du Noüy suggests. But—his ultimate purpose? I do not think anyone knows more about that than I know, and

I know nothing about it.

Your greatness is here and now. Your happiness is here and now. Here are some of the factors which create peace of mind. They are involved in creating money-wealth as well; but let us set that aside for the time being. Here are some peace-of-mind factors; read them carefully; note that you have met them in this book, in one form or another, and note that you have heard about them from other sources as well.

You must come to realize you have a conscience which will guide you, and stay on good terms with your conscience so it will guide you well.

You must take possession of your own mind, do your own thinking, live your own life.

You must keep yourself so busy living your own life that you will not be tempted to interfere in the lives of others.

You must learn to free your life of unnecessary encumbrances, both material and mental.

You must establish harmony in your own home and harmony with those among whom you work.

You must share your blessings with others, and do this wholeheartedly.

You must look at the realities of life as they are, not as you wish them to be, and properly evaluate them.

You must help others to find and develop their own powers to make themselves what they want to be.

Now, I did not invent these ways of winning peace of mind. They were known of old. They are the ways which have proved themselves right, strong and eternal. If I have made these ways more clear to you, and if I have given you practical ways in which to apply them, well and good; but the wisdom behind them is the gathered wisdom of mankind.

And so you have heard before of these peace-of-mind

factors. Perhaps they were told to you as ways to help yourself get to Heaven. This belief leaves you up against a blank wall. I give them to you as representative of the tried and true methods which help you live a healthier, wealthier, better life, here, on this earth, now. Is this not sufficient?

The Creator in your life. You have seen that I do not deny the concept of a Creator as an eternal and all-pervading intelligence, or cosmic force. But the Creator with whom I made my peace many years ago does not require me to be afraid of Him; nor does He offer Himself to me merely through the intervention of any particular religion.

My Creator gave me His greatest blessing when He made me human.

He gave me the power to choose between good and bad, and made my concept as wide as all the affairs of the world and all its people. He set me at large upon the world to learn that my good deeds are rewarded in kind, and my bad deeds are just as inexorably made to draw penalties according to their nature. He gave me a mind beyond the mind of any other of His creatures, and He made me free to use my mind as only a human being can use his mind-power.

I can pray, and in constructive prayer that does not amount to begging for special favors. I can find faith which vastly enlarges my powers. Yet always I know I am the master of my fate, I am the captain of my soul, for so my Creator made me, and so I need not call upon Him constantly for guidance. Have you ever noticed that the one who does the praying very often has a large part in the answering of the prayer? I allow for the prayer that goes Beyond; but I believe that many a prayer stays within the one who prays and strengthens him in his realization of his own human abilities.

The Creator's place in your life is to help you be more

triumphantly your own master. The Creator made you a creature who can think for himself, be himself, believe in what he wishes to accomplish, and mightily achieve! Do less than this and you cannot possibly fulfill yourself in all your glorious humanity.

The mind of man is filled with powers to be used, not to be neglected. These powers, these blessings, either are used—and the benefits of their use shared with others—or you incur penalties for not using them.

If you needed a house, and knew how to build a house, and had all the materials you needed for building a house, and had a lot on which to build a house, and yet neglected to build a house—then you would understand your penalty as you sat exposed in the rain and the snow.

Too many of us do not use our power to gather in the wealth and peace of mind which is available all around us. Then we are penalized by poverty, by misery, by worry and ill health—and we blame everyone but ourselves.

Anything the human mind can believe, the human mind can achieve.

Believe in poverty and you will be poor.

Believe in wealth and you will be rich.

Believe in love and you will have love.

Believe in health and you will be healthy.

You have seen what lies behind these statements. It would be well to read this book again and refresh your understanding. No book can give you all its wealth at the first reading. Make friends with this book, read it again, put it away for a while, take it out and read it once more, and you will read much between the lines—and much that applies to you.

I have shared with you what may be merely words, or great wealth and contentment—depending on how you use them. I am glad I cannot force you to use the knowledge I have given you. I am glad it is up to you to improve your own life.

I leave you now with no great ceremony.

Remember: There is no good thing in the world that is not available to you if you sufficiently desire it.

And remember: No matter what others may see of your possessions after you make a great deal of money, no matter how they may respect your offices and influence and talents no matter how much they may admire your generosity, your kindliness, your willingness to live and let live . you yourself are the only one who can hold and enjoy your greatest treasure, peace of mind.

Cherish your visions and your dreams. They are the children of your soul, the blueprints of your ultimate achievements.

POINTS TO REMEMBER

1. Fear has no place in a well-lived life.
2. Peace of mind, the greatest of the riches, and how to find it.
3. Find the power to turn what the human mind believes into what the human mind achieves.

www.ingramcontent.com/pod-product-compliance
Lightning Source LLC
Chambersburg PA
CBHW032230080426
42735CB00008B/789